TURNING WORDS INTO WINDOWS ®

US:

A COLLECTION OF OUR STORIES, THOUGHTS, AND DREAMS

ISBN: 979-8-9899598-3-9

To the ones who paved our paths,
the ones walking by our side,
and the ones who will dream the future...

VOICES

Aidan
Alana
Alex
Alexandria
Alexis
Angie
Anthony
Anthony M.
Arinze
Ashley

Audriane
Aye
Aynul
Cameron
Ceceilia
Chris
Christina
Darius
David
Demi

Dennis
Drew
Edison
Emely
Emma
Gabrielle
G. Evelyn
Hala
Irene
Jamie

Jasmine
Jazzy
Jenna
Jeremy
Jodi
Joshua
Jovan
Joy
Juan
Julia

Kam
Kobe
Kyle
Kyle B.
Lanre
Liam
Liz
Marvelous
Michael
Morgan
Najee
Natalie
Navin
Nia
Nicole
Omari
Pamela
Pat
Piero
Philippa
Priscilla
Samira
Sharod
Shevin
Sondrea
Steve
Sue
Tabitha
Tina
Travis
Tyler
Victoria W.
Vishhel
Zoe
Zoe M.

//CONTENT #01

NOTE FROM THE AUTHOR	05
INTRODUCTION	06
UFAFANUZI WA MASHARTI Definition of terms	07
CHAPTER 1 The Black Experience	10
LIVING IN TWO AMERICAS PT. 1	26
CHAPTER 2 The Allied Voices	28
CHAPTER 3 Calls To Action	40
LIVING IN TWO AMERICAS PT. 2	50
CHAPTER 4 Reflections, Hopes and Dreams	56
MY STORY OF TRAUMA	62
GEORGE FLOYD 2 YEARS LATER	66
OUR LOST VOICES	70
US	72
JAMEL OGBONNA Purpose Through Music	74
DAVE THE BARBER	78
IZDIGO: SOUTH ORANGE'S VERY OWN	80

NOTE FROM THE AUTHOR

From the Garden City of Georgetown to the Big Apple of New York, I've spent most of my young life writing and bringing stories to life. I believe a great story is a window to a world unknown, allowing you to see life from a different perspective.

Turning Words Into Windows® was created for this purpose: bringing stories to life and offering a look at the lives of real people. The blueprint for this remaster of the inaugural issue titled "US: A Collection of Our Stories, Thoughts, and Dreams" was originally published in July 2020, and focused on the issues of racism and societal injustice faced by the Black community. It featured voices from around the world. Two years later, these stories and the world they reflected remain unchanged.

To everyone in this book, I thank you again for trusting me to share your stories with the world in 2020 and sharing these stories now. Each of your stories left an indelible mark on me, and gave me hope knowing that around the world, regardless of gender identity, race, and geographic location, we were and still are committed to speaking up despite not walking in each other's shoes. With this book, we have truly turned words into windows.

-Daniel C. Haynes

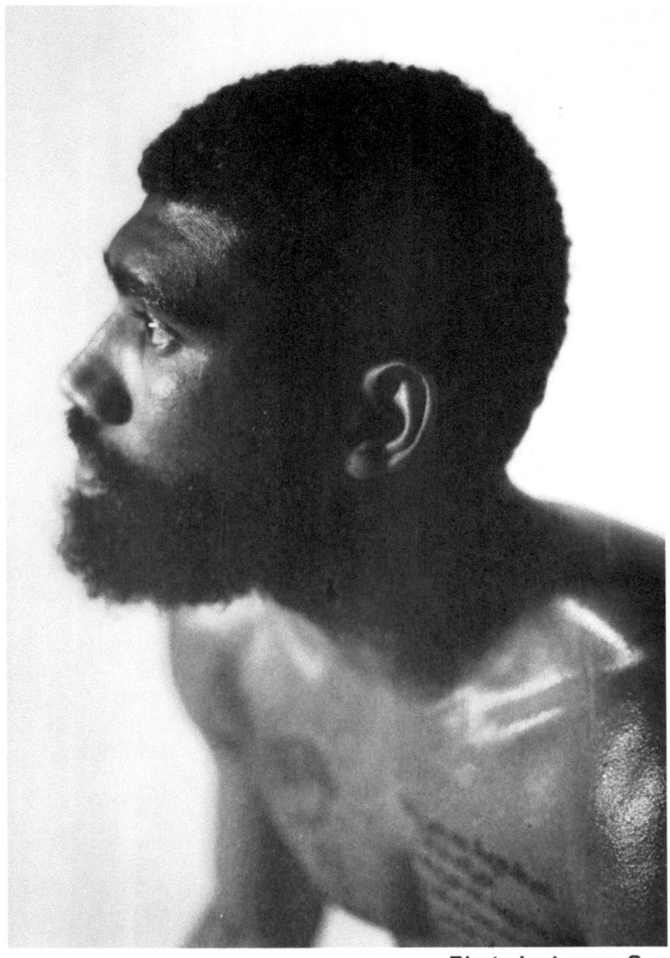

Photo by Luana Seu

INTRODUCTION

"One day our descendants will think it incredible that we paid so much attention to things like the amount of melanin in our skin or the shape of our eyes or our gender instead of the unique identities of each of us as complex human beings."

-Franklin Thomas

In the United States, "One in every 1000 black men will die at the hands of the police" (Edwards et al., 2019). While this statistic is alarming, the issues of racism and social injustice faced by the Black community do not begin and end with police brutality.

These issues are interwoven into the fabric of our daily lived experiences from the day we open our eyes when born, to the day they close either naturally, or are forced shut by the police. They're in every sigh of relief we breathe as patrol cars pass after appearing in our rear-view mirrors. They're in every prayer said before leaving home and the unspoken emotional release that comes when you do make it home.

They're in the systems that were never designed to support us in a country **our** backs were whipped to build. In the flooding of **our** community with drugs, the policies designed to limit and deny **us** resources in our communities. They're in the prison to pipeline system unjustly incarcerating **our** men and women.

On May 25, 2020, the world watched in shock, disgust, and anger as the murder of George Floyd in Minnesota at the hands of police played over the airwaves.

"I can't breathe," Floyd said, reminiscent of Eric Garner who said it 11 times before being murdered by police on July 17, 2014.

Breonna Taylor was murdered in her home at the hands of officers executing a no-knock search warrant on March 13, 2020.

Ahmaud Arbery was murdered by white men after being racially profiled while jogging on February 23, 2020. Trayvon Martin was murdered on February 26, 2012, because he was wearing a hoodie. Tamir Rice was murdered on November 22, 2014, while playing in a park with a toy gun. Eight years later May 24, 2022, police failed to fire their weapons at a mass shooter who took 21 lives including 19 students and two teachers at Uvalde High School in Texas.

Their names are only a few in the ever-growing list continuously (being) written with Black people's blood.

Over the next few pages, the experiences, feelings, stories, and dreams of Black people will unfold. You will see their pain laid bare, and as you read their stories, reflect on how their lives and worth have been determined by the amount of melanin found in their skin. You will also read the stories of allies using their privilege to add their voices to the conversations of change long overdue.

Thank you, and welcome to:

UFAFANUZI WA MASHARTI

(SWAHILI, DEFINITION OF TERMS)

In the conversations surrounding race and the Black experience the words, phrases and terms used in these conversations are often misunderstood. The definitions on this page are to help frame your understanding of the words and experiences found in this book. They are taken from the Meriam-Webster Dictionary.

African American: An American of African and especially Black African descent.

Allyship: An active, consistent, and arduous practice of unlearning and re-evaluating, in which a person in a position of privilege and power seeks to operate in solidarity with a marginalized group of people.

Black: The term Black generally refers to a person with African ancestral origins. In some circumstances, usually in politics or power struggles, the term Black signifies all non-White minority populations. The term Black has a long service in social, political, and everyday life and in its use to denote African ancestry, and in its use to denote African ancestry it is entrenched in epidemiological and public health language.

Discrimination: The intended or accomplished differential treatment of persons or social groups for reasons of certain generalized traits. The targets of discrimination are often minorities but they may also be majorities, as Black people were under apartheid in South Africa. For the most part, discrimination results in some form of harm or disadvantage to the targeted persons or groups.

Ethnicity: This refers to the identification of a group into a "people". This distinctiveness is believed to be expressed in language, music, values, art, styles, literature, family life, religion, ritual, food, naming, public life, and material culture. This cultural comprehensiveness- a unique set of cultural characteristics perceived as expressing themselves in commonly unique ways across the sociocultural life of a population- characterizes the concept of ethnicity. It revolves around not just a 'population" or a numerical entity, but instead a "people," an all-inclusive unique cultural entity.

Institution: A society or organization founded for a religion, educational, social, or similar purpose; an established law, practice, or custom.

Nappy Hair: Nappy hair is specifically used when speaking about the hair of Black people although textured hair goes by many names like curly, kinky, or coily.

Prejudice: An adverse opinion or learning formed without just grounds or before sufficient knowledge; an irrational attitude of hostility directed against an individual, a group, a race, or their supposed characteristics.

Race: The idea that human species is divided into distinct groups based on inherited physical and behavioral differences.

Racial Passing: This is when someone's features cause them to be mistaken for another racial or ethnic group.

Racism: Racism, also called racialism is any action, practice, or belief that reflects the ideology that humans may be divided into separate and exclusive biological entities called "races" and there is a casual link between inherited physical traits and traits of personality including intellect, morality, and other cultural and behavioral features leading some races to be innately superior to others. It is without scientific basis.

Slave: A person held in forced servitude.

Slavery: The state of being owned by another person; the practice of owning slaves.

Social Injustice: Social injustice is the unequal treatment of a group within a society, which results in one group being at a disadvantage.

Social Justice: Social justice is the view that everyone deserves equal economic, political, and social rights and opportunities.

System: An organized set of doctrines, ideas, or principles usually intended to explain the arrangement of working of a systematic whole. Also, a form of social, economic, or political organization or practice.

Systematic: Presented or formulated as a coherent body of ideas or principles.

Systemic Oppression: This is the intentional disadvantaging of groups of people based on their identity while advantaging members of the dominant group (gender, race, class, sexual orientation, language, etc.)

Black Lives Matter Protest: New Jersey
Photo by Isaiah Gill

CHAPTER

ONE

THE BLACK EXPERIENCE

IN THIS CHAPTER WHAT IT MEANS TO BE BLACK IN AMERICA WILL BE FULLY EXPLORED. THE THOUGHTS AND STORIES YOU WILL READ ARE FROM BLACK PEOPLE BY DEFINITION, RACE, AND ETHNICITY.

"Honestly, why? Why must Black men and Black women continuously be treated like animals in this country? Why do the police constantly take pride and joy in antagonizing us brothers and sisters for absolutely no reason at all?

Why do they see the color of our skin and automatically think "thug" or, "criminal?" Why has this country never been in favor of African-Americans? It's as if we only matter when we are dunking a basketball, scoring a touchdown, or making the next best song. I don't understand how this country continuously treats us the way that it does. I am beyond numb from everything that's been happening. It definitely leaves a great level of confusion in me. When Trayvon Martin was murdered in cold blood, I was 14 years of age.

I'm 22 years of age and here we are on the same book, just a different chapter... I will never understand how America can look at a certain person and treat them worse than garbage. But I do know how resilient we (Black people) are. I do know we are the ones who built this country from the soil up and we are not going anywhere. I have so many questions about the tactics and the methods this country uses to exterminate our brothers and sisters. It's almost like they do it purely out of pleasure.

All I can ask is why... Why?"

-Aidan, 22, Georgia
June 1, 2020

"With everything going on I don't know how to feel or who to be mad at. I'm pissed at every cop that's ever taken a Black person's life, but at the same time, I'm mad at my people for taking each other's lives. RIP Pop Smoke, RIP Nick Blixky, and RIP KJ Balla. How can we expect cops to protect us when we don't protect each other. Change starts from within. We have to be the change we want to see."

-Omari, 23, Flatbush Brooklyn
June 2, 2020

"The past week has been very difficult for me. Watching the video of George Floyd's murder was a horrific experience, but I feel it was necessary. Floyd's public lynching is an example of how Black people in America have been treated for generations. We can be completely innocent, not resist, beg for help, and still be killed in broad daylight by the people sworn to protect us. It is evident that there are systems in America that do not protect or apply to us. We are not criminals, we are not animals, and we are not destructive.

Although this has been a very depressing time for all of us, it's amazing to see the Black Lives Matter movement become global. People are finally seeing that this is not just an "American" issue, but a worldwide one. Black Lives Matter EVERYWHERE. Seeing the unity of many different cultures, religions, and races showed me that this is no longer just a movement or a protest, but a revolution. We are witnessing history."

-Anthony, 20, New York
June 2, 2020

"It's everywhere. From the time you wake up, we begin the struggle that is being Black. I must watch what I'm doing all the way down to the way my feet move when I walk. Even when I do everything right, will people march for me or justify my death? Take the power back; don't wait for that elusive handout. Now, they must "Look at my African Americans."

-Kyle, 22, The Bronx
June 2, 2020

"I hope that everyone understands that this isn't just about George Floyd. It's years of not being heard, people's lives being taken from them over and over, and having to educate generations that the America they live in is different from some of your friends and greater community. We have tried every way for the people in power to hear us. I pray that change can begin with the conviction of Floyd's killers and keep going until I don't have to think that my skin color can limit my opportunities or be the reason why I died. "

-Alex, 19, Michigan
June 2, 2020

"US": A COLLECTI

Black Lives Matter Protests in Detroit
Photo by Lamar Price

"Growing up I went to all white schools and lived in all white neighborhoods, so it is not hard to guess that I dealt heavily with my own deal of racism, discrimination, and even identity confusion. The first time I can recall someone saying something racist to me, I was 5 years old. My sister and I were playing in a jungle gym with other children until one of the children told us we couldn't both play because one black kid was enough.

In first grade we had 'chocolate day' in our class, where we all tried different chocolates. When I got to the table with white chocolate, I was told I wasn't allowed to sit because I was black and only white people can have white chocolate. On the bus in the fifth grade, I was told I couldn't sit in the front of the bus. In 10th grade, my teacher told me I would probably score lowest on my AP World History because "that's just statistics."

In 12th grade, nearly every day, I was called the n-word, called a monkey, a gorilla, and plenty of other derogatory names. No one condemned any of the students involved. You often hear that racism will fade out because this generation is "past racism". But it is not. Racism still thrives in the mentality of those people who are in the same young generation as I because it was taught to some. While not everyone grew up that way, there are still many who did. So, we cannot rely on racism getting "phased out" because it is still flowing through our younger generations.

Black people have endured 400 years of racism, oppression, discrimination and enough is enough. George Floyd was not the first, but he was the final straw. The Black community is sick of hearing about the loss of another one of our Black brothers or sisters; we are tired of wondering "Am I next?"

Black people are killed by law enforcement at exponentially higher rates than any other race in the United States. Not only is this an issue of police brutality, but Black people are also under attack from the government. So, we need reform not only throughout the judicial, but also the legislative and executive branches. The legislation was not and is not written in the interest of protecting Black bodies; and 45 does not care about protecting any other race other than white. This is why it is important to vote. We cannot thrive in a system that was never built to protect our rights. A combination of standing up, using our voices, protesting, and voting is the way to get the justice we deserve."

-Kam, 22, Brooklyn
June 4, 2020

ION OF OUR...

"It's a struggle some of us have had to deal with. Until you've witnessed it for yourself you will never understand. Now I'm very privileged to have lived in America and the UK where I currently reside and have experienced my fair share of racism. From employers taking liberties and giving preferential treatment to non-coloured counterparts because they can, being on nights out and being subjected to drunken racial slurs; to people passing comments on the interracial relationships, I choose to be in...

I've heard things like you guys come here to steal our girls, why don't you stick to Black girls, stick to your own kind... The list goes on!

What I do know is nobody is born a racist, this behaviour is learned. I've been racially profiled by police, wrongfully arrested, and even mistreated while in police custody.

But I ain't about to cry about it, as one of many in my position, we just gotta deal with it. At this time in my life, my mental state is solid, people's opinions and perceptions of me isn't my problem or responsibility and quite frankly I don't care. Opinions don't pay my bills. It's as simple as that. I have not a single fuck to give! If you know me, you already know this.

Then to top it off, wade in the "I'm not racist, my cousin's brother's sister's friend is Black", or the "All Lives Matter" brigade! No one is saying all lives don't matter. The best analogy I've seen elsewhere is: if a person's house was on fire and someone was trapped inside, "Are you gonna make the fire department go to every other house on the street first because all houses matter???" NO!

What's sad is that at some point I'll have to explain to my innocent beautiful little girls that, in life, some people WILL dislike/hate them because of the colour of their skin and that breaks me. IF we were appreciated as much as our culture is embraced then we'd be further down the road perhaps... Who knows! At least we are now having that conversation.

Besides that, though, being BLACK is LIT.
#BLACK AND PROUD"

-Kyle, 32, Hull United Kingdom
June 5, 2020

"Over the last few days, everything that has happened is heart-wrenching. It was heart-wrenching to see how casually George Floyd's life was taken, how minorities, particularly African American lives are continuously seen and treated as insignificant. It aches my heart that as African Americans, we have to go to this extent to be heard, that the names of Black men and women have to become a hashtag in order to be seen as a victim, when years of systemic racial discrimination and oppression have already made us victims. I understand the riots. I understand the frustration. I understand the fear. I understand the anger. I also understand how hurt brings out solidarity not just among African-Americans, but also among those brave and willing to stand up to injustice, inequality, and the public lynching of Black lives.

Change is necessary and it should at least start with law enforcement accountability. We are wearisome of political pledges and promissory police changes. My career within the Department of Justice solidifies my belief that there is no excuse for lack of accountability. If the justice system would also consistently and swiftly hold them accountable, then and only then justice is allowed to prevail."

-Alana, 25, West Palm Beach, Florida
June 5, 2020

Black Lives Matter Protests in Detroit. Photos by Lamar Price

Black Lives Matter Protests in Detroit Photo by Lamar Price

Black Lives Matter Protests: Washington DC

"I grew up with a distrust for police and white people based off my skin. At age 12, I had the cops called on me for trying to get my dog who ran off—leash in my own neighborhood.

As I grew up. I noticed that this issue was much bigger than just having the cops called on you for being Black - you can be killed. All my actions have to be like walking on eggshells when walking around police. Even around white people a situation in which I am the victim can be made to look the other way.

Black people have been portrayed in a bad light by the media for far too long. I believe that Black people should be rioting. We have held our emotions in for far too long. It's hard, it is extremely hard to be alive as a Black man in this country, and no one tries to make it easier for us.

We can be called a nigger to our faces and the only thing we can do is eat it. That's it. Everything else is considered wrong by law. We have been discriminated against for far too long and it needs to come to an end whether it be peacefully or not."

-Dennis, 21, Queens
June 6, 2020

"Our world once again has seen more African Americans die at the hands of the police. Enough is enough and the world is letting it be known. To be a Black man in America should be something you are proud of but it's not.

From a young age I was told that I live daily with two strikes against me: being Black and being a Black male. I soon realized what they were telling me. I have had moments of being followed around stores; being told I should be happy I was allowed to be in certain schools. I've been stopped by the police and questioned on how I can afford my car.

I've had a gun pointed at me because I fit a description. I've not been promoted to positions because they said I didn't have the necessary requirements while white co-workers with less education were in higher positions. I've not been compensated appropriately for all the work I was doing. This is what being Black in America has meant to me.

As I raise a Black son in this world, I am committed to doing all I can to ensure that his future does not reflect my current realities. Our world needs healing, our world needs peace, our world needs togetherness, but what the world really needs is truth and honesty! The TRUTH that it has not done right by African Americans. We are born with aspirations and goals to succeed in life, not to be the world's next statistic."

-Sharod, 37, Lefrak City NY
June 6, 2020

"I'm tired. I'm really tired of explaining to my white friends how important it is that they advocate for Black lives every day, not just when it's a trend on social media. I'm tired of having to prove that racism is real.

I'm tired of seeing so many white people get huge praise for standing up and saying the right thing, when really that should be expectation. I'm tired of seeing the appropriation of Black culture without the defense of Black lives.

I hope that the effort I'm seeing from my non-black peers on social media is the same effort that they bring to the table when they're chatting with their family members or friends and hear a racist comment. I hope that the volume and intensity of this fight continues even are George Floyd's murderers are found guilty. Most of all, I hope that at the end of my life I can look back and see some real progress in this fight so that my own children are better off."

-Zoe, 21, Maryland
June 6, 2020

Black Lives Matter Protests: Philadelphia.
Photo by Caleb Johnson

"There is a misconception that due to Connecticut's history of being a blue state, we don't have any pressing issues associated with race, or that we just aren't like that. A sign posted just ten blocks from my house reading "Black Lives Matter" has been torn and cut down three times now. Followers of the town's Facebook page claim it's the fault of heavy winds, but in reality, the action was fueled by blatant, unjustifiable racism.

As I prepared myself for a peaceful protest at the capitol building this week, my mother offered to add her creative touch to one of my Black Lives Matter posters. She began to add green craft glitter to the emboldened letters. As she decorated, my mother asked me why I hadn't thought to use the poster I had made five years ago in my high school art class. Honestly, I had no idea what she was referring to until she brought it over to me. As I dusted the surface, the memories returned.

The year was 2015. Our class assignment was to create an artistic public statement representing a specific cause that we were passionate about. It was early April, social media and news outlets had just begun depicting the horrifying murder of Freddie Gray.

The year is now 2020.

The oppression is the same.

My heart aches the same, the tension still remains.

It pains me that this five-year-old poster is still relevant. In 2015 my passion went to the extent of creating a poster for a grade. Today, I stand actively with my community to dismantle systemic racism and bring light to lives lost due to police and human brutality."

-G. Evelyn, 20, Connecticut
June 7, 2020

"The murder of George Floyd at the hands of law enforcement was one in a long list of many. For me however, it was a first.

It was the first time I didn't want to post about it, or tweet about it, or talk about it. I couldn't watch the video. I blocked it all out. I was, and am, tired. At some point I had allowed myself to become numb to incidents like these because the pain and hurt had become too much to process.

As days pass, I find myself in a constant state of anger. I am angry that we have to beg to be seen and heard. I am angry that our mere existence is perceived as a threat. I am angry knowing that it will be a good while before things change. After all, how can we fix a system that wasn't built with us in mind? An intricate system that was built to intentionally oppress us. I don't want to dismantle the system anymore; I want to build our own.

Don't wait until it happens to someone you personally know for you to begin caring. Even in my numbness and anger, I won't allow myself to become complacent or distracted. We are asking for the bare minimum: equality. And it's not so much that the ignorant don't know but rather that they don't want to know. Why would they protest a system that benefits them?

So, my current mood: calling everybody out on their bullshit. My pigment doesn't dictate my worth and I refuse to be silent."

-Aye, 22, East London
June 7, 2020

"The sun was scorching that day. I lived in Orlando, but it was especially warm. I raced from one end of my high school to the other hustling to make sure I wasn't tardy. The cool air hitting my skin was a welcome relief as I entered the building where my class was.

As I approached the room, I heard a voice say, "You there, you're out of dress code." I looked around and saw a heavy-set white woman, one of the teachers, pointing at me. I thought, it couldn't be me. I was wearing a blouse and jeans today. She looked at me again and said, "Stop, you need to go to the office."

My heart raced because I'd never been sent to the office. I'd never skipped school or been to detention. In confusion I responded, "Why? What did I do?" She pointed to my arms and said I was wearing a shirt with no sleeves, a clear violation of the rules. I hadn't realized in my haste to get to class on time my short sleeves had rolled up under my backpack straps.

I pulled it out to show her and tried to explain but she cut me off abruptly and told me again. My cheeks felt hot in embarrassment. I walked to the office where I tried to explain that this was a misunderstanding, but I was issued a dresscode violation t-shirt to wear. It was hideous.

An unsightly neon oversized t-shirt to let every single adolescent soul know I was out of dress-code. I felt humiliated having to wear it the remainder of the day.

The next day as I walked to class, I saw her chatting with some other students. They were the popular girls in school. I noticed their ivory skin and miniskirts as she told them they looked cute today. I thought to myself, "Why didn't she send them to the office for dress code violation?" Skirts that short were in clear violation of our dresscode.

In my naivety it took me a moment to fully grasp what had happened. Suddenly I realized the rules were different for me because of my darker skin. In the weeks to come my mother scheduled a meeting with the administrator and the teacher.

She brought along her friend, another white teacher who agreed with her lies

Black Liv

ves Matter Protests: Washington DC

when she told us all that I had been wearing a sleeveless shirt that day. My mother walked out fuming and feeling powerless as the school administration sided with the teacher. My face felt hot again. Tears poured out.

As I walked out, I turned to the administrator and said "This is not fair. You know it isn't right."

-Jamie, 32, Orlando Florida
June 7, 2020

"I was 12, my white teacher kept trying to prove that I was cheating on exams because I was doing really well. I kept outperforming one of my white classmates whose dad funded the school. She also confronted me about being 'smart'. She im- plied I had to be 'mixed' with something besides black because I was really smart, and my skin wasn't like a Black person's. Eventually, she was reprimanded by the principal of the school after my parents reported her."

-Vishhel, 22, New York
June 8, 2020

"Why should being a black man be paramount to being born cursed. It scares me, that at any given time, my time can be up. Being in the wrong place at the wrong time, or even being in the right place at the right time but facing someone who is racist. I carry this fear every day of my life walking in a hoodie, whenever I see white police officer, I take it off so they can see my face clearly.

I take my hands out my pockets, so they don't think I'm hiding anything. I hate that this is the world we're living in, especially in the 21st century. As a Black man with a white woman, I've also seen hate perpetuated by our own people. Why am I with a white woman? Why am I betraying my own kind by not being with a Black woman. I think this, and any narrative like this also perpetuates hate towards our own.

I often wonder how I will explain to my children who will be biracial, that the world is a cruel place. How do I help them navigate the world as biracial Black men or women. I've also experienced colorism and seen us fight our own based on who is light skin versus dark skin. It may sound counterproductive, but I believe until we can accept each other regardless of whatever differences, we won't be able to unify and fight this. I love my people, and I'm thankful for those allies who are lending their voice to an issue that has plagued our community over hundreds of years."

-Chris, 24, Grand Cayman, Cayman Islands
June 9, 2020

Black Lives Matter Protests: Washington DC

Black Lives Matter Protest: Detroit
Photo by Lamar Price

"As a Black woman, I'm 99% sure that we are subjected to racist acts whether physical, verbal or not, at least once in our lives. Whether we are Black, Yellow, Red... I've seen and heard people criticizing someone just because he or she is Chinese, Brazilian, American... I myself treated someone badly because of his nationality or his origin and insulted him when I was younger...

I'm not proud of it but I've grown up and I understood that it did, it does, and it will always hurt. There are so many types of racial acts, but to kill someone? It's the limit, the dirtiest level someone can reach. It's the most horrible way there is to harm. Moreover, to use your uniform or your job to achieve ends like willful death is a horror. By practicing acts like this, you dirty your jobs but also the WORLD and especially the human race. The world is us, not racism, and it's not Black people against racism, it's the WORLD against racism.

Peace and love."

-Audriane, 24, France (72)
June 10, 2020

"As a light skin Black person, I am afforded a few privileges my darker skin brothers are not, and I have never learned it better than when I was on a cruise from Oslo, Norway to Copenhagen while on vacation in 2017, Denmark. I had to take this cruise because I didn't realize how far both cities were from each other, and I needed to get to Copenhagen the next day.

I was sitting at a counter at the "night club" of the ship drinking a Brooklyn Lager when I was approached by a Danish man, who instantly knew by looking at me I was American. "Who are you?" he asks. I tell him I'm from New York traveling across Scandinavia. He was so excited to talk to me he bought me another beer. In general, he was a fun guy who loved life.

When the conversation turned to American politics, things took a dark turn. He exclaimed right in my face, "people like Barack Obama because he was a good nigger president. He showed me niggers could do good things too." He said to me—to my face. I spent the rest of the night wondering if I were a few shades darker, like my brother and sister, how he would have treated me. I wondered if these were the kind of conversations white people had about us behind closed doors.

If this is how they see us, do they even think of us as human? Will they ever see us as human?

Needless to say, I had another drink... or three."

-Juan, 30, New York
June 11, 2020

"Every time I see something like we saw with George Floyd I always think about my dad and my brother. It always hits personally for me. I know that they have a harder time than me being Black men in America. I am scared every day that my dad may not come home.

I live in a predominantly white neighborhood. I have a Black dad and a white mom. So, when I was younger, I would always notice people stare at my family whenever we went out to eat. As I got older, I started to realize why this was happening. There weren't very many interracial couples in my town growing up.

Also, when I go out with my mom and sister, people always assume that my sister was my daughter. While these are small things they begin to add up over the years. One of the biggest things that I have experienced when it comes to race is that people always ask, "What are you?" While I know that they mean, I have always found this question so insensitive. It's hard enough being mixed and not knowing which group you will fit into.

I'd rather not have to explain it to everyone I meet. I am so happy that people are finally starting to speak out and demand justice for Black people in America and all over the world. We have already seen that things have begun to change which shows that protesting and signing petitions works."

-Victoria W. 20, West Palm Beach, Florida
June 12, 2020

"

Many people don't realize how hard it is being a Black individual in America, let alone a Black man! Over the years, I've personally felt equality has been overshadowed. I am already prejudged prior to having a conversation with, interviewed, or even stepping foot in a room. I find it quite exhausting to walk around in my 10.5 shoes; if you cannot relate to the injustices Black people face daily.

When your influence is too big, they assassinate you. And when you keep it too real, they fabricate who you are and what you stand for... I've seen this happen too often. But now is time for all to set the precedent and stand together to fight for what's right, which is human rights!

Everyone puts their pants on the same daily, so no one should be perceived as being superior than others. And, we cannot say All Lives Matter until the world appreciates Black Lives.

-Jovan, 30, Louisville, Kentucky
June 12, 2020

"I was very young. About 18 or 19 years old and I travelled to Wisconsin for the first time to participate in the cultural exchange program 'work and travel'. I was placed at Bobbers Island Grill to work, this was five (5) miles from where I was given a housing. I would ride my bike for about an hour in the morning before I could get to work. This morning I speak of was very cold, in fact it had snowed a little.

I was riding my bike and a red car drove pass with white folks inside barking like dogs, I laughed. Little did I know that was a racist thing to do in Wisconsin and that it was derogative because racist folks saw Black people as dogs and would attempt to communicate with us in "dog's language." I continued to work unbothered, remember I didn't know that was a racist move.

I fell off my bike and got badly hurt. No one, absolutely no one assisted. They all kept going about their business (these were all white folks). I started to wonder if it was just a different culture because had it been in the Caribbean I would have been assisted. Little did I know that it was because I was Black.

I arrived at work late because I had to walk the rest of the journey. I did this while in pain because I was badly injured. I was hoping that when I got to work, I would get assistance to go to the hospital. This didn't happen, instead, I was told to go drink some water [and get to work]. I immediately quit my job and asked the sponsor to send me home. They apologized and assisted me in finding a new job at Kickers, now closed. The experience was wonderful thereafter.

I have now grown to love America, but my experiences have caused me to be in full support of the BLM movement."

-Travis, 23, Wisconsin
June 12, 2020

"As I sit here to write on the morning of my 22nd birthday, I do it in the same room where exactly one year ago I stood crying in disbelief I made it to the age of 21. My experiences have led me to the realization that as a Black man in America, I had a target on my back, and every day I wake up is a blessing.

I remember sitting around the TV with my family and watching Trayvon Martin's murderer get a non-guilty verdict. I remember being the only Black kid sitting in classrooms in high school on several occasions where this country's weaponization of my Blackness was the topic of discussion. Even in my so called "progressive" hometown there was no form of proper discourse to ease the minds of young Black men and women. This evidently led to half-assed attempts by my school district to have Black students 'educate' non-Black teachers more than twice our age on our plight and how racism affected us daily.

In the summer of 2014, I immersed myself in the Black Lives Matter movement monitoring protests through Twitter and Periscope to get firsthand accounts of how the police were responding to peaceful protesters demanding to be treated and respected as citizens like our non-Black counterparts. All of this took place before I reached the age of 18.

After high school, the state sanctioned murders of unarmed Black men and women by police didn't stop, neither did the media's exploitation of Black Death. Things hit home when my uncle pleaded with me to cut my dreads while I was a sophomore in college because he feared that my hairstyle would add to the probability that I would get killed by the police.

Above I've only mentioned a fraction of experiences during my childhood that warped my reality. I was always taught that as long as I do what is right, "Dress the right way", and "Speak properly", I would be okay. As a recent college graduate, I have no more tolerance for respectability politics. I thank God everyday unapologetically for my Blackness and our culture. Quarantine in combination with the murders of Ahmaud Arbery, Breonna Taylor and George Floyd may they rest in peace has led me to confront a lot of my trauma that was subconsciously suppressed. It's on my generation to make a difference, the world needs our leadership now more than ever. I don't subscribe to the notion that all cops are bad people but as an extension of a corrupt institution that currently serves to uphold and enforce white supremacy. Instead of protecting and serving citizens, they are proponents and benefactors of injustice.

As I reflect on the privilege it is to have reached another year of life, I understand that this is also another year of opportunity to do something meaningful. If there is even a sliver of a chance to form a future where my kids won't have to grow up carrying the burden that weighs on Black men and women of this country and world today, it's something worth fighting for. True and impactful widespread change isn't going to come from the system that exists. This system is broken because it continues to deny Black men and women justice for being wrongfully murdered and persecuted because of the color of their skin. Change has to come from the people, it's not black vs. white.

This isn't about politics.

It's about how we treat each other and an acknowledgment that we can live in a society where equity and compassion are the norm and not reserved for people of a certain skin color or creed over all others."

-Lanre, 22, Amherst, MA
June 13, 2020

"During this time around the world, we have come to a point where staying quiet and walking by is not enough anymore.

I think that this was needed because there are people in those uniforms are white supremacists and who soil the whole thing they stand for. That makes me look at all people with those jobs a different way because it turns me to believe that at least one or more persons has to know that you are one. Which makes it like they are taking each other's back with this topic which isn't right because no person with hatred in their heart would ever do the job correctly.

I feel like it also ends up the worst for people of color because we are the people that they envy. We are the people they hate because of how we are built, look, and talk. That is so sickening because none of us would even go to bother them. They will literally come and harass innocent people which starts to make you look at the police as a gang more than a protective force for us. I think now is the time when we start to weed out the supremacists from their hiding place in the office and encourage them to leave or retire. This makes room for the next generation of cops being officers who actually like to interact with Black people."

-Pat, 21, Haverstraw, NY
June 13, 2020

"The recent events have led me to do some soul-searching. It pushed me to think about topical issues I had side-tracked because of life. It is truly disheartening to see what is happening to the Black race out there; racism is a reality to most if not all.

It should never be that I can't browse a store freely, or that I am automatically deemed white because of how I articulate myself. Let's not even talk about systematically where advisors reduce my intelligence and try to convince me to not push myself to my fullest capabilities. It's crippling to know that every time I step outside, I might not make it back in.

Sadly, that's the reality of being Black in America."

-Jodi, 20, New York
June 13, 2020

We all remember the first time we were called a racial slur, "nigger". It was a Thursday afternoon at the Leigh High mall in Pennsylvania with a group of friends. We were coming back from a field trip; I was 14 at the time. We were walking around the mall when this old white man walked by us and said it under his breath, "niggers". I stopped; did he just say that? It was so weird to me; this was my first time experiencing blatant racism.

This man had to be in his late 60s and he just called a group of children "niggers". I wasn't angry, I wasn't sad, I wasn't hurt, I was humored. F**k that guy, he's probably dead now anyway and if not, he's probably clinging to life. I wonder if there's a place in heaven for people so ignorant, I hope not.

Wait, maybe that's a little harsh. Maybe ignorance is all he ever knew, maybe he's a product of his environment, as am I. Maybe he's weak; of course, he's weak. I forgive that man and I appreciate him for showing me that everyone isn't for me. Luckily it was just a slur; for Ahmaud it wasn't just a slur, for Trayvon it wasn't just a slur. A change must happen, and it must keep happening.

Unfortunately, I won't reap the benefits of what we're fighting for today. However, maybe when I have kids one day, they will. Maybe I won't have to tell them that there are people who will judge or hurt them because of their beautiful Black skin."

-Darius, 23, Queens, NY,
June 14, 2020

"Racism has been tattooed into my life since I was born. Going to predominantly white institutions which were perceived to have the "best education" failed to leave out why they were considered the best. Attending private catholic institutions comments like "you could be a slave", "your hair is too nappy", "you're not pretty because you're tan" are words I grew up hearing. At a young age I knew these were offensive phrases. My "best" education showed me how racist their institution was every single year I attended. A major ex- ample is being assigned the role of a slave in the school play along with the other Black children.

Racial injustice must be put to a stop. We must stand tall and fight and reform the system. I worked in the streets fund-raising for the ACLU to fight for basic human rights and fight against ignorance, systematic racism, and instilled prejudice.

Raising thousands of dollars for lawsuits to be filled against Trump and racial injustice lawsuits did not come without hardships. Every single day I would canvass in front of the White House getting verbally abused by Trump supporters. Enough is enough. We demand justice now."

-Jasmine, 20, Maryland
June 14, 2020

"Because we have seen the murder of yet another Black person due to racism.
Because I have to explain to my children that they may be looked down upon regardless of what they do.
Because people who signed up to defend our country, often from low-income backgrounds, will be forced to exert force or risk losing jobs.
That people are hurting and are responding to that hurt through violence and destruction because their voices are unheard.

I'm angry.
That it took so long for charges to be filed.
That in some cases charges haven't been filed

I'm scared that...
individuals hired to protect us can
hurt us without consequence.
Children will be exposed to even
more violence and sickness as a result.
There are those who seek to profit
off of the pain being displayed,
through violence and manipulation.

I worry that...
The protests will cause a resurgence
in COVID cases, costing more lives.
That scare tactics will force us to
return to the status quo.
That demands are not stated and
will not be met.
That young people will be charged
with crimes that will negatively
impact their lives forever.

I'm hopeful...
that leaders will emerge from this
action that will inspire a
generation and create meaningful
and sustained change.
that there is more goodness than
evil, and more love than hate.

I question...
My privilege and complicity with the
status quo. I wonder if I am doing
enough.
What justice looks like.

I'm shocked that ...
Violent, coordinated attacks are
occurring and are not fully
investigated.
I'm prayerful...

For the families who have lost
children to racist actions, whose
pain has been used and
manipulated for positive change
and for violence.
For our nation.
For our children."

-Ceceilia, 39, Queens New York
June 14, 2020

Black Lives Matter Protest: New Jersey
Photo by Isaiah Gill

LIVING IN TWO AM

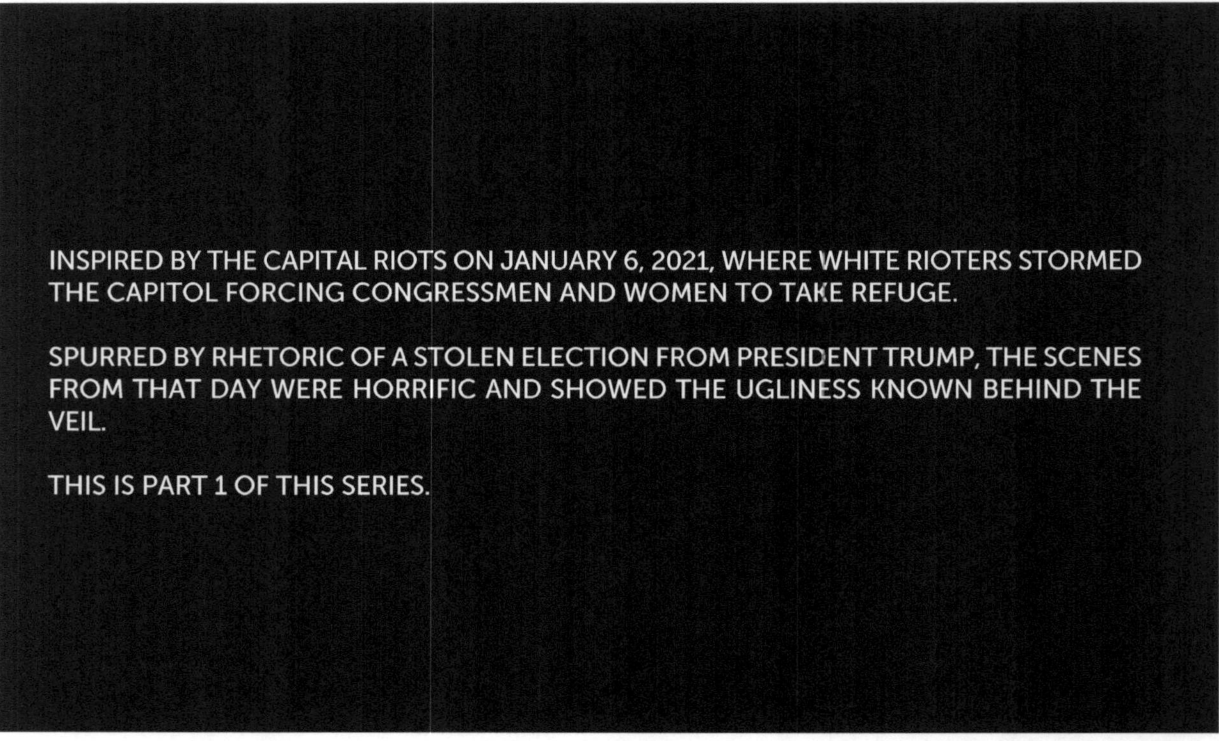

January 8, 2021,
New York

It has taken me days to process the way I felt watching Wednesday's events play out, and now [3] days later I still grapple with the events. To see hundreds of white rioters take the Capitol reinforced what I and millions of Black people already knew: We live in two vastly different Americas.

For white Americans, America is a place where they grow up instilled with the confidence to destroy Federal Property, scale the walls of the Capitol Building with rope, and not fear the police. For me and the millions who look like me, it's a place where every day is spent with anxiety thinking it could be your last just for existing. If you think I'm being over-dramatic look at last year: Ahmaud Arbery (25) was chased and shot in his back while out jogging, Breonna Taylor (26) was shot while asleep in her home. George Floyd (46) was murdered for allegedly having a fake $20 note. A murder that was re-enacted by two white supremacists during the white riots.

Atatiana Jefferson (28) died in front of her 8-year-old nephew when officers were responding to a call saying her front door was open. Police unloaded 20 bullets into Stephon Clark (22) while he was in his grandmother's backyard holding a cellphone. The list of Blacks killed by the police and/or racists is unending.

Looking back at last summer when the Black Lives Matter (BLM) protests were taking place, peaceful

ERICAS PT. 1

Written by Daniel Haynes

protesters were shot with rubber bullets and sprayed with pepper spray. They were left with throats burning while choking on the smoke of tear gas. They were left running away from police with tears pooled in their eyes. They were zip-tied and forced to lay on their faces on streets and sidewalks.

They were protesters marching against racial injustice and systemic oppression. But, for the police, that wasn't the right way to protest. Yet years, before, Colin Kaepernick kneeling during the national anthem was also not the right way to protest. What is the right way, one wonders? Was what we saw on Wednesday the right way? The police were informed about BLM protests and were clearing streets, out in riot gear and ready to be cruel. The president tweeted out instructions to the supporters and the energy from the police was lethargic.

I am not advocating that anyone be shot with rubber bullets or pepper sprayed by the police when petitioning for their rights. What I am asking is that we be afforded that same gentleness from the police. And what we saw on Wednesday was not a protest for rights. It was sedition. But, in that America, even when they storm the Capitol in an act of insurrection, white people are still helped down the steps.

How can we see the wide gap in treatment and not recognize the competing Americas? If you will not treat white people the way you treat Black people, will you treat us the way you treat them?

Black Lives Matter Protests: Philadelphia.
Photos by Caleb Johnson

CHAPTER 2
THE ALLIED VOICES

ALLYSHIP. IT'S A TERM THAT IS COMMONLY USED IN THE CONVERSATION OF SOCIAL JUSTICE, BUT WHAT EXACTLY DOES ALLYSHIP MEAN? WHAT DOES IT MEAN TO BE AN 'ALLY'? IN THIS CHAPTER, STORIES OF ALLIES WILL BE SHOWN. THE BRIEF DEFINITION BELOW IS TAKEN FROM 'THE ANTI-OPPRESSION NETWORK'.

"ALLYSHIP IS NOT AN IDENTITY—IT IS A LIFELONG PROCESS OF BUILDING RELATIONSHIPS BASED ON TRUST, CONSISTENCY AND ACCOUNTABILITY WITH MARGINALIZED INDIVIDUALS AND/OR GROUPS OF PEOPLE. "

STORIES OF ALLIES CAN BE FOUND IN THIS CHAPTER. THERE WILL BE NO IDENTIFIER OF RACE OR ETHNICITY, UNLESS STATED BY THE ALLY THEM-SELF. YOU CAN BE AN ALLY, REGARDLESS OF GENDER IDENTITY, RACE AND ETHNICITY, OR AGE.

THE QUESTION IS, WILL YOU?

"In recognizing the humanity of our fellow beings, we pay ourselves the highest tribute."

-Thurgood Marshall

"I've been looking at this for 30 minutes trying to come up with something to write, something to express how I feel, trying to put my feelings into words.

Coming to America from The Bahamas, I have NEVER in my life seen racism like this. My heart breaks for my best friends, my boyfriend, my co-workers, my boss, my colleagues, my Black brothers, my Black sisters, and AMERICA.

I know I will never understand what you feel or what you have to go through on a daily basis, but I stand with you. George Floyd, Ahmaud Arbery, Anthony Harris, Dason Peters, Ryan Stokes, and so many more. I am sorry for the justice system.

I am dumbfounded that, yet another Black man had to die for America to finally wake up.

I am disturbed and disgusted that this has happened. I am distraught that everyday Black people fear for their lives from people who are supposed to be there to "protect" them. It is disgraceful that to this day, TO THIS DAY, this still continues.

But we cannot be silent, we cannot sit here and pretend that this isn't happening. "Our lives begin to end the day we become silent about things that matter." -Martin Luther King Jr.

-Zoe M. 20, Nassau,
The Bahamas
June 2, 2020

I'm not Black. I can't pretend to know what it feels like to be fearful of those sworn to protect us. I can't say I've ever been mistreated or made an example of. I can't change the hearts of the Americans who have denied and upheld systematic racism.

But I have felt heartache, sickness, pain, and empathy as I watched racist men and women take the lives of George Floyd, Ahmaud Arbery, Eric Garner and many others.

My place isn't to tell you how to grieve. My place isn't to tell you how you should protest. My place is to stand with you, support you, and see this through to the end. "Justice will not be served until those unaffected are as outraged as those who are."-Ben Franklin

-Jeremy, 24, California
June 3, 2020

"Being from Detroit, I know firsthand what animosity and injustice from the police force towards Black people can do.

The city of Detroit itself still hasn't fully recovered from the race riots of 1967, where one of the bloodiest incidents of the confrontation between Black residents and the Detroit police department occurred.

What's going on now is a rehashing of those very incidents. The fact that almost 60 years has passed and nothing seems to have changed is telling of American society. The fact that we haven't evolved past the need to routinely treat Black people and other people of color as lesser than us says a lot about the values that many people in America hold- even those I grew up with around Detroit.

The fact that we allow the police force—a job that is meant to protect and serve all citizens of the United States—to repeatedly demonize, attack, and even kill Black people and other minorities is something that can no longer stand under any circumstances. The lack of accountability held by police officers, our elected officials and even your racist neighbor, is just one of the many catalysts for this uprising and push for equality.

Many of these overtly racist people in America are quick to misquote things like the Constitution and Declaration of Independence, or continue to praise America for its equality, yet always seem to dodge this one very important quote that was a building block to their oh-so-great country: "All men are created equal."

Until this actually rings true for not only white Americans, but all American citizens, especially those that are Black, this civil unrest is beyond justified."

-Piero, 22, Detroit, MI
June 3, 2020

"If you're white and you have to imagine being oppressed to feel guilty or upset about what's happening, that's a problem. Being a person is about more than doing the daily things of brushing your teeth and checking the mail.

It's realizing that other people are suffering and hurting because of who they are. It's caring about your neighbor, the person who doesn't have enough fare for the metro or the person in class who needs a pen because they forgot theirs.

I was raised in a white household in a community of Black and LatinX people. Being raised in this neighborhood of minorities and poverty we tried to support each other. Supporting one another was what we lived off of.

I personally am mixed, "white-passing" with a Black father and a white mother. I was always too white for my Black friends and too Black for my white friends. But being mixed and Black is a part of my identity.

I know that my voice will never be ostracized or doubted for the color of my skin, but I still feel so much pain for the Black people around me for my Black family because what is happening right now has been going on since before the history textbooks could erase it.

And I want to continue using my white privilege, my empathy, and my voice for people in the Black community because it's the right thing to do and because they're my family.

I'm sorry if you think I don't have a say in the matter, but I feel like I do. I will always step aside for the Black community whose voices NEED to be heard, and I will always uplift them, but I just want to take this moment to share my pain and to urge white people to use their privilege to do the same. To fight for those who are being shot and killed for just driving or walking down the street. To donate.

To just fucking care about the injustice.

And at the end of the day, if you're white and can close your eyes at night and feel like you're doing enough, you're not.

Black Lives Matter.

These people matter.

We with privileges should always use the power that we have, to let their voices be heard."

-Alexis, 22, Maryland
June 4, 2020

"Growing up in Philadelphia, I was not blind to injustice. Yes, I am fortunate, but I am not sheltered. I was taught from a young age about what is right and what is wrong.

What is happening in our country today is blatantly wrong. Racism is the endemic. It has taken YEARS of fighting just to achieve equality... And we don't have it yet... In the year 2020. It is extremely important that everyone does their part. If you don't know how, look up some resources, books, articles, music, art... Anything to help you learn and aid you in taking action.

What does not help is turning a blind eye and ignoring what is happening in the world around you. It may not directly affect you, but that is no excuse to back down from the fight. We must stand together."

-Anna, 20, Philadelphia
June 4, 2020

"Growing up it was instilled in me to see the beauty in the world. Lately, I found it nearly impossible to. How can there be any beauty in the world when my Black family, friends, and community is being murdered for their complexion?

There is no beauty in that well the beauty comes in the unification of communities coming together to fight for Black lives. As a white-passing Latina, I acknowledge my privilege and I promise to utilize it to help and progress Black lives.

The anger we feel should be nationwide and though it is not, we must use that fuel our fire for justice, for peace. We need real leadership in our administration, not a coward hiding through this. We, the people, hold the power as a collective because together we are strong, and we have proven that.

Now is the time to reform. One last thing I've noticed myself [doing] is telling people "be safe, or stay safe out there", instead of "have a great day..." let that sink in."

-Irené, 21, Imperial Valley
June 5, 2020

"I'll never fully grasp the systemic racism that exists in the US because it's different for us here in Guyana and the Caribbean. That should make it even worse if I could nonetheless recognize its existence.

I see the pain, the oppression from this system and what it has inflicted on minorities, especially Black people and I fully understand the rage their showcasing now. I might not fully get the destruction and looting, but if that's how the message has to be sent over, so be it, can't blame 'em."

-Michael, 22, Guyana
June 5, 2020

"For to be free is not merely to cast off one's chains, but to live in a way that respects and enhances the freedom of others."

-Nelson Mandela"

Photo by Luana Seu

"US": A COLLECTI

"I am white, I grew up in a white town. I believe there were approximately 5 Black girls at my all-girls Catholic school any given year that I was attending. In short, privilege runs through my veins.

Moving to Queens, New York was a culture shock to me. It was a learning opportunity. Many of my classes allowed for me to hear the differential experiences of people around me. Outside of school I loved to explore the city around me and experience new places and learn about the people that lived there.

One night I ended up in a situation that could've ended up very differently for me were it not for the color of my skin. I was arrested for shoplifting, something that could've easily been avoided if I had simply asked my parents for money. Many people that shoplift don't have that option, that luxury.

I did it for a thrill. I was taken into custody where I was held in a cell until it was time for my intake.

While the officer took my fingerprints, the machine wouldn't register my prints and it took many tries and a lot of time. The entire time this was happening, the officer and I were joking, laughing, and relaxed. He even made me giggle before my mugshot.

The recent press about George Floyd's death made me reflect on this time. If I was not white, this would not have been my experience.

If I was not white, my charges could've been more severe.

If I was not white, that cop would not have been as nice to me.

If I was not white, I could've died.

It is my duty to acknowledge the injustice in our judicial system. It is my job to bring awareness and make a difference.

I am not Black, but I hear you. I see you. And I will not be silent."

-Emma, 21, San Diego
June 6, 2020

"The recent events around the murder of George Floyd sparked outrage in the nation.

The first time I REALLY noticed this country had such a huge racial issue was in the 8th grade. Trayvon Martin, 17, was murdered and my friends were divided on whether or not his killer deserved to be in jail.

This was pretty foreign to me cause all my life I was taught killing is wrong no matter what. People were saying things like "Why was he in that neighborhood at night," and, "Why didn't he just do what the man asked?" And I was confused.

But this wouldn't be the last time I heard people I love making excuses for killers and it definitely would not be the last time I questioned humanity.

There have been too many Trayvon Martins in this country who have died viciously and unjustly, and no one has been held accountable.

As I've grown, I've learned more about the Black Lives Matter movement through experiences and the people I've surrounded myself with. I've had conversations with family members, and people I've looked up to for years, that turned to arguments over the movement.

I am sick and tired of turning the news on and seeing the same thing over and over again with no changes besides a new organization being founded or a new street name.

I won't be caught watching anymore, this is not a Black issue, this is a human rights issue and to say it's not is beyond ignorant.

I am tired of being scared that if my friends are out late, or in the 'wrong' neighborhood they won't make it home.

This is a revolution, and it won't be silenced."

-Jenna, 21, Hackensack
June 7, 2020

ON OF OUR...

"I have not experienced what the Black community has, but my heart goes out to all of you, and I will continue to fight alongside you forever.

For years and years, rights were designed, systems were built, and they were claimed to be for everyone. But "doesn't apply to Black people" is written in the fine print. The judicial system and those in positions of authority are marketed as the ones who are doing the protecting, when in reality, they're the ones people need to be protected from.

I feel that people were not taking this situation seriously for years up until now. People could use racial slurs and their defense would be. "I don't use it with bad intentions", then, there are others that have been silent regarding these issues because it doesn't affect them and thus it isn't their problem...

Even now, some people are silent, ignorant, and avoidant. I've experienced so much ignorance from some of the people I've spoken to. People would say that their, "discomfort" prevents from speaking out.

Some people would explain that they don't usually do this, so it feels a little off to start now. People go on and on and say, "I just don't like to talk about this." But it is a conversation that we must have.

In just these last few days, I have seen the growth in strength of people when we stand together. I hope everyone goes beyond the limitations that they set for themselves. Protect and support Black owned businesses, donate as much as you can, sign petitions, make that call, send that email, and vote. Protect and support each other."

-Hala, 19, Brooklyn, New York
June 8,2020

"I live in a conservative household on Long Island. Growing up, I was taught many things by my family, one of them was that depending on your race you were predetermined to be a certain stereotype and the other was that anything deviating from the American white picket fence and nuclear family with a mom and dad was wrong. In my primary school these ideas were reinforced. The school was Catholic and the students within the school were primarily white. There were a few people of color to interact with and students were generally fed similar racist narratives by their families.

Although my bias was something I wasn't entirely aware of at the time, I knew that the beliefs we were fed weren't to be trusted. Part of my distrust came from my own identity as a gay man. Because I was seen as gay before I knew I was gay,

I was bullied from a young age by the same majority of white people who willingly believed and acted on the racist rhetoric of their parents. This pushed me away from them and the structures that reinforced these beliefs. So, I gravitated to the students in my school that were also pushed aside, this included other people of color in my grade who were socially segregated from the general population.

I made an active effort to escape the environment of Long Island as I became more aware of my sexuality and the consequences I would face if I remained. I went to a school in Manhattan I knew very little about on a scholarship where I was lucky enough to be plunged into a different world. People were more accepting of not only me, but also people of color, and talking about race in critical ways with knowledge I was only exposed to online.

Hearing the experiences of Black people in the Spectrum group, a group focused on race relations, made me more aware of how police brutality and racial profiling, (something I never encountered due to my privilege), were topics that teenagers my age had to reconcile with.

The implicit bias I grew up with was continuously challenged and rewritten. Many people do not understand implicit bias, or think they are immune. It is a strong, instinctual, and unavoidable part of the subconscious that is reinforced by media and microaggressions we see in daily life.

I have the privilege of being able to hide my sexuality from my family, but Black people cannot hide the color of their skin. They are forced to deal with racism from an early age while other children can remain blind or run from their problems like I have.

I still seek to undo the years of internalized racism and homophobia.

I still seek to question authority.

And I still seek to make sure that in my future profession I understand how my own implicit bias can affect how I treat patients in the healthcare system, and how racism influences the disparities within it.

Changing law enforcement is only part of the solution, every part of society must be remodeled not only to exclude racism, but actively fight against the bias it was created with."

-Anthony, 20, Long Island
June 8, 2020

"One of my earliest memories of racism is when I was in 4th grade and being teased by my siblings about my new "boyfriend" (I mean, does one really date at the age of nine?).

We were at my grandfather's house having dinner. My boyfriend was Black, and his name was of Haitian origin. As they teased me, my grandfather asked what was so funny, so my siblings told him about my boyfriend. My grandfather replied, "That sounds like a n----r name." It was the first time I heard the n-word, and it is etched into my memory even now—28 years later.

Even though I didn't know what it meant, I knew right away that it was wrong. I knew because my mother immediately interjected and said "Dad, you can't say that. Don't talk like that in front of my kids."

I am now the parent of two girls. I remember how important it was for me to witness my mother confronting my grandfather on his use of a racial slur. I now find myself doing the same thing for my daughters as they listen to our neighbors and certain family members attempt to make racist jokes, condemn rioters, and question protesters. I speak out every time.

I've focused much of my efforts during the recent unrest to challenge the white parents in my circle and my local predominantly white school district to educate children on race and to practice anti-racism.

The children of the world are watching and like little sponges they are soaking up your emotions, your words, your actions, and your silence. What are you teaching them?

Oh, and my 4th grade boyfriend by the way... We've stayed close friends to this day celebrating birthdays, weddings, and births together for 28 years and counting."

-Sue, 37, Long Island
June 9, 2020

"So, I have never truly had a run in with racism, the closest I've been were experiences in America because my voice didn't match my skin in certain people's eyes. One might say that, in itself is some sort of privilege. I have, however seen many occurrences or have heard stories from very close friends about their run ins.

The thing that this entire situation really brought to my attention was how skewed my view on police brutality in America was. Regardless of whatever country I was in or lived in, my experience with law enforcement has gone from just nor- mal to quite pleasant but this gave me the hard reckoning that it was my experiences that were the one offs, and the shared experiences by everyone else were the norms.

These series of events really showed me how genuinely justified black people in America, and hell all over the world where this fuckery occurs, are in their fear, frustration, and anger. They have been ignored for far too long and this response, as we are starting to see now, is and was the only way to bring about any semblance of change.
There is one other thing that this movement has made me realize - the number of people that I shamelessly kept as a friend or associate or simply just tolerated being around, knowing fully well that when they're behind closed doors, or with like-minded people such as themselves, that they were racist.

It's really fucked up to know that right now, amidst all this amazing change, the conversation in the households and friend circles of those people are more along the lines of either property dam- age, supporting the police, or that mindlessly stupid response of "all lives matter."

-Navin, 24, United Kingdom
June 9, 2020

"The cost of liberty is less than the price of repression."

-W.E. B Dubois

"In recognizing the humanity of our fellow beings, we pay ourselves the highest tribute."

-Thurgood Marshall

"I became aware of the Black Lives Matter movement back in 2015 when Sandra Bland had died because of police brutality. Since before and after the movement began, there have been countless incidents where Black people have died from police brutality.

Without video proof of these people getting killed by police, imagine the amount of people that were murdered because of racist cops with no justice being served. I am glad to see the movement receive massive amount of attention and importance that it has always carried. The media has portrayed the protests to be violent, created a false narrative. The protests do not represent the looters, or the people vandalizing, the protests represent the innocent

Black people who have died from police brutality. It is because of these protests that governments are trying to make change. I am optimistic that change will happen, and I am glad to be a part of the generation that is fighting for justice. George Floyd, Breonna Taylor, and the countless of other Black people that have been unjustly killed by police deserve justice.

Racism is something that should be addressed everywhere. Ahmaud Arbery was racially targeted and murdered while jogging through a neighborhood by racist white men. Black people in America have faced racism and oppression ever since this country was founded. This is not only with po- lice, but in every profession that exists.

I hope that after we get change with police brutality, there will be change in dismantling systemic racism. It is important we all acknowledge it and learn how greatly it has affected Black people. We all should be open to educating ourselves about the injustices that Black people have faced and continue to face.

As for me, I will continue to do everything in my power and beyond to advocate for and protect Black lives and will always be open to learning how I can be an ally and a friend to my Black brothers and sisters."

-Nicole, 19, Queens, NY
June 9, 2020

"One week ago, I graduated from the University of Toronto with a Bachelor of Applied Science in Chemical Engineering. However, that didn't matter a week ago and it still doesn't matter a week ago and it still doesn't matter today because the BLM (Black Lives Matter) community is where OUR focus should be.

Growing up as a mixed individual (including African Guyanese) has definitely opened my eyes to all the racial difficulties that exist in this world. I've only experienced it from just being a spectator, either with my family or friends.

But I have felt those eye-piercing stares that weren't for me. I have felt the fear caused by those stares. A fear that leaves you anxious and wondering what is gonna happen next. It's appalling and should not even exist. I only feel that fear when I'm with them, but they feel that fear every second of every minute, of every hour, of every day, of every month, of every year of their lifetime, wherever they go, which is unjustifiable, cruel, corrupt, unethical, immoral, and just goddamn wrong.

To all my African Guyanese, African American/Canadian friends and to my family, please know I stand with you till the end.

P.S For those of you that chant "oNe pEoPle, oNe NaTiOn, oNe DeStInY" all over your Facebook every Independence Day, Republic Day or whenever something great happens for the "Guyanese people", don't chant it if you're not willing to pull up and support your people who are in dire need right now."

-Gabrielle, 22, Toronto, Canada
June 9, 2020

Black Lives Matter Protests: Philadelphia
Photos by Caleb Johnson

"I am not a Black person in America. But I am not a white person in Australia either. My grandmother and father immigrated to Australia from Peru. My mother's parents immigrated from Greece. My family understands the racism that they experienced, but I struggle to get them to understand why #BlackLivesMatter. "The darker you are the poorer you must be." I remember hearing that so many times growing up. Marrying well was marrying someone whiter than you.

It hit home when a few years ago, I saw one of my close friends, a Chinese exchange student, apply white foundation powder to lighten her face. In Asia, just like in Peru, if you have dark skin, you are associated with rural poverty, from a bloodline of ancestors who spent their days working under the sun. I could never understand this. That having dark skin is (STILL) something people are made to feel ashamed of. It blew my mind. I could not believe that college-educated people my age, in my family, were so conditioned by racist colonial language and ideology, designed only to estrange and oppress minorities.

I love Black culture and I did my best to empathize with Black struggle. But I quickly learned that this is nowhere near enough. Studying in New York a few years ago, I took every opportunity to learn about structural racism, institutionalized racism, 'white fragility' (DiAngelo) and how by not being Black I had an advantage.

I care a whole damn lot about Black and non-white Americans. They showed me so much love, and for no reason. People who I now consider close friends, invited me (practically a stranger) into their homes, to eat and stay with their families. They shared with me, their first-hand experiences of what it is like to be Black in America.

All I had to do, as a non-Black person was shut-up and listen. I guess that's a function of my privilege, much determination, innovation and entrepreneurship, despite a suffocating and oppressive system that still enslaves African Americans (physically and psychologically). What I learned and witnessed myself, made me feel that Black people really have to be exceptional (an artist, rapper, director, actor, politician, etc.) for white people to treat them with common decency as fellow human beings.

That is wrong.

It is my duty as a non-Black person, who goes about life with so many freedoms, to educate other non-Black people who still choose to be ignorant. People who deny the existence of racism and white privilege are not my friends, so it is never a comfortable thing, to call people out and have confrontational conversations about race and systemic racial discrimination, to have to prove that Black lives are valuable lives.

But it is a whole lot more comfortable for me than it is for a Black person to have the same conversations with the type of white people I'm referring to. I used to cut people off for being racist, now I realize that removing myself, does nothing to better the issue. It's just me turning a blind eye. Every single day, I am learning more and more about what I can do too, just the same, I am learning all the things I need to stop doing."

-Tabitha, 23, Sydney, Australia
June 10, 2020

"As a white woman who was raised in a predominantly white neighborhood, I know that I have always benefited from white privileged.

As a child, this privilege was never something my parents or teachers explained to me. I think this blatant ignorance says a lot about how the majority of white parents and schools do not properly educate children on present-day racist inequality.

Thinking back to high-school, I remember our principal releasing a statement to inform us that Black Lives Matter t-shirts were not permitted in school. The next day, the ban caused a divide between students who supported the BLM movement, and those who preached that "all lives matter."

A public school, funded by the taxes of Black families and minorities in my town, not only took away free speech, but also attempted to cover up the inequalities between students. It is ridiculous that these same types of "all lives matter" people from all over the country have gone through years of school and still preach an uneducated rhetoric.

We are in an age where it is so incredibly easy to educate yourself by reading articles, Twitter threads, or even Instagram captions. THERE IS LITERALLY NO EXCUSE. No matter how you were raised, continuing to support a movement rooted in institutionalized racism makes you ignorant and racist.

I will continue to have tough conversations with family members who I know do not feel the same way as me, because there just aren't any excuses for racism."

-Ashley, 19, Pittsburgh, PA
June 11, 2020

"These past couple of weeks has been a wakeup call for America, finally. I come from an Iranian American and I'm considered white. So, I can't share my experience of what I've been through myself, but what I can do is use my voice, which a lot of people in this country need to do better.

America was built on being free, being equal and having a voice, but why does that not apply to African Americans and other minorities? This country was not built by white people, there is no history on white people and their culture so why do they feel the need to oppress people who did build and make this country?

It makes me so angry that people can't see what's happening here. The people who don't see the need for change are blind, are flat out selfish, and they will, and need to be called out. The government of this country needs to be called out as well.

There are so many problems that they have turned a blind eye to, and I hope that they can finally wake up, but it starts with us. Keep protesting, keep speaking out, and don't be silent.

Don't be upset because you feel like this problem doesn't to you... Be upset because it's happening in the country that is supposed to be number one'."

-Samira, 22, Maryland
June 13, 2020

"Being a white male, I am privileged to not have my livelihood in danger when encountering police officers. Right there, what I just said, is the problem at the hand.

People should not be excluded from having the privilege to know that the police are there to protect and serve solely because of the color of their skin.

I stand in solidarity with those who unfortunately must fight just to be heard so that they can live in a country that recognizes their rights.

I will never fully understand the injustices that so many Blacks have to face, but I hear you and I'm fighting with you."

-David, 21, NY
June 13, 2020

"Racism isn't born folks, it's taught. I have a two-year-old son. You know what he hates? Naps! End of list."

-Dennis Leary

Black Lives Matter Protests: Philadelphia
Photo by Caleb Johnson

"With everything going on in the US right now you can definitely see everyone's true colors if you couldn't before. I am white, I have never felt, and will never feel the racism that so many people feel on a daily basis. Some choose to not acknowledge this because it makes them feel better about themselves.

I have never feared for my life when seeing a police officer, and never has anyone been afraid of me due to the color of my skin. I have seen a lot of people using metaphors to explain the situation in simple terms for the more hard-headed people who oppose the Black Lives Matter movement.

I myself even used it the other day to try and get someone to understand. But to try and take away the suffering people are feeling and dealing with every day at the hand of institutionalized racism and police brutality is selfish and cruel.

How can some stand by and ignore the evidence right in front of them. I don't think the metaphors are working, I think the people who don't support the movement don't want to and we all know why.

Those who say, "blue lives matter", and "all lives matter" are really saying white lives and white cop lives matter more. Hearing my grandmother say this didn't surprise me at all since she has plainly stated once that she was glad my little brother broke up with his girlfriend because she didn't want him dating a Black girl.

Hearing this confused me to the point where I thought I was hearing things. We were in a restaurant, in public she said this for others to hear. That's when I knew I didn't care if they were mad at what I was saying, I was always going to use my position of privilege to speak my mind for those who can't.

People need to get over the uncomfortable feeling and speak. Use your voice and your privilege, otherwise what are you good for. It's extraordinarily simple in my mind.

Either you're racist, or you're normal".

-Tina, 23, Long Island, NY
June 15, 2020

CHAPTER 3
CALLS TO ACTION

Calls for continuing social justice action can be found in this chapter. Each voice standing in solidarity, represents what we can achieve when we work together.

Ending systemic oppression, as well as standing up for what is right, is something we all need to do, regardless of our gender identity, age, religion, race and ethnicity, or geo- graphic location.

The issues of police brutality, systemic oppression and racism are human rights issues.

If you're unfamiliar with what social justice is, or simply need a refresher "social justice means the rights of all people in our community are considered in a fair and equitable manner", (Meriam-Webster).

There are four interrelated principles of social justice; equity, access, participation, and rights."

"**Equity:** to ensure fair distribution of available resources across society."

"**Access:** ensure all people have access to goods and services regardless of age, gender, ethnicity, etc."

"**Participation:** Enable people to participate in decisions which affect their lives."

"**Rights:** to protect individual liberties to information about circumstances and decisions affecting them and to appeal those people feel are unfair."

"Everything that's going on right now is necessary. For years and years, we have been treated unfairly and have had to deal with the pain of this horrible treatment. We've done the hashtags, the peaceful protests, etc., and it's honestly gotten us nowhere.

So, when we are continuously being ignored and seeing that these peaceful protests aren't doing a damn thing then we gotta go about it a different way to make people feel us. Also, when you're at these protests, make sure to not hurt any Black owned business that has looked out for us and helped the black community through the years.

Never hurt those that help you and that are there for you. Remember Ephesians 6:11-12 "Put on the whole armour of GOD, that ye may be able to stand against the wiles of the devil. For we wrestle not against flesh and blood, but against principalities, against powers, against the rulers of the darkness of this world, against spiritual wickedness in high places."

-Tyler, 22, Georgia
June 1, 2020

"Well, if it's one thing, I happy that we showing up injustice. Black people really have been through a lot and all we are told to do is to turn the other cheek as Christ said to do. But enough is enough. The judicial system don't really care about colored people, as a matter of fact, it's there to oppress. So, I sat and really focused on this thing, stayed quiet and meditated. It really have some countries and other nations going through much worse. Little Muslim girls being raped, stoned and if she ain't dead by then? They put her out in the open surrounded by about 15 guns and shoot her mercilessly.

What America facing is only bad based on American standards, and this kinda proves that almost no place safe. Any system built on broken policies will eventually fall and the astronauts that left earth yesterday made the right move at the right time. Cause I just wish it had a planet for me to go to, or even a star to sit on to be away from all the ills of humanity."

-Kobe, 20, Trinidad and Tobago
June 1, 2020

"I was born and raised in the Caribbean, but I came to America for a college education. When I first came, I didn't fully understand and agree with everything that my friends of color were warning me about.

As the years went by, I VERY QUICKLY understood everything they said, and changed my thinking on many subjects. Watching on TV truly is not the same. It's time for change! To my brothers and sisters on the outside of America, we must support in any way we can. This fight is not just their fight, it's our fight as well."

-Jazzy, 22, Trinidad and Tobago
June 1, 2020

"I've never been to a protest. Frankly I am scared to go to one. The news only shows the violence that comes with a protest. Therefore, I struggled to process what was going on in America.

I knew the cause and the reasoning for this movement, but I still felt as if I was in the 2020 age watching a movie with a 1900s plot of the world fighting for equality. It seemed far from me. But I was uneducated. I was inexperienced. I was viewing the cause as an outsider, even though I am not. To learn I listened to hours of podcasts, read poems, watched videos, and immersed myself in the constant posts from trusted sources. Social media became the place I found where it was important to voice opinions.

As I posted, more and more of my white friends showed their support and asked questions, confirming the importance of activism on media. I can't wait till I get the chance to walk along side of thousands of protesters fighting for the same cause. The sense of community I've seen amazes me. I love all my people that show support and act in love. Black lives matter. We need justice. Let's change the world."

-Julia, 19, Willowgrove, Pennsylvania
June 3, 2020

"These last few days have been emotionally draining, seeing all of the injustice against our black people day after day. For hundreds of years, we've been treated like less than human beings simply for the color of our skin. Our own police, the people who are supposed to protect us are actually the ones brutally beating us, killing us and racially profiling us on a regular basis. It's wild that when I see an NYPD car, I actually feel more scared than put at ease.

But then again, why am I surprised? They're enforcing laws that were never meant to defend black people, but instead neglect them and their needs while continuing to uphold and instill the values of a white supremacist society.

People are upset with the looting and the protesting, well, our people have protested peacefully for years and what has it gotten us? So now, we're gonna MAKE SURE you hear us. Outside of black owned small business, I feel bad for not a single multi-billion-dollar corporation that got looted, they'll get it all back in a day.

Please, continue to protest. If you can't do that, donate money. If you don't have any to spare, sign a petition. If you don't have access to the internet, call your local government leaders and DEMAND CHANGE. If you can't do that, simply just educate yourself on the problems that our community face every single day. Don't become complacent in fighting to end injustices against black people, if we become silent, they win."

-Najee, 21, Queens, New York
June 3, 2020

"I've been to two protests regarding systemic racism in America and both times I felt angry, heartbroken, frustrated, and exhausted. I wanted to yell loud enough that people heard the pain in my voice, loud enough that they heard my dedication. We targeted our chants based on what we saw, if I saw a group of white people on the sidewalk just recording, I'd yell "WHITE SILENCE EQUALS VIOLENCE." If I saw a bunch of cops, "HOW DO YOU SPELL MURDERER? NYPD!".

I am going to continue to yell and protest because I want this country to know we see its corrupt, racist ways. We are tired of asking to be seen as equal, but we will continue to demand it because that's what we deserve.

BLACK LIVES MATTER!"

-Nia, 20, Brooklyn, New York
June 4, 2020

"I'm terrified to speak. Terrified that somehow my words will be used against this movement or be seen as apologetic to those who revel in oppression and subjugation. But I know that, like in art, truth sometimes comes from the places we most fear. And so, I want to share in my fears so that maybe we can find hope.

I'm scared that this movement will just be another in the history books. That children will be taught it but never fully realize the significance of it.

I'm scared that this movement will push us apart, drive a deeper wedge in the world and threaten to pull it apart until one side is alive and the other is dead.

I'm scared that the people I love in my life are in danger because of the colour of their skin and that one day even my whiteness will not be enough to save them from oppression. And most of all, I'm scared that stories do not matter anymore.

I want to believe in stories. I want to believe that if people just told each other their experience that maybe empathy would breach the divide. I dream that maybe a person of colour's story might resonate with a single white person and cause them to see beyond rhetoric, beyond physical differences.

And yet it seems that only through violence and division that change truly occurs. That stories have no place in wartime and that this is, in fact, wartime. That the role of storytellers is dead to the need for survival. And that the only solution now is to fight until blood is shed."

-Liam, 24, Canada
June 4, 2020

"I swear to the Lord, I still can't see,

"I think what is taking place in America is very pertinent and should be seen, noted, and supported by ALL black persons globally. It's very personal and very distressing to see persons, who look exactly like myself fighting to live, to be seen, to breathe.

Colonialism and slavery have ingrained and cemented these systemic racist ideologies that continually haunt and diminish the significance of our blackness. It is time that we acknowledge this, break down the system and rebuild it so that equality comes out on top in order to protect the lives of black men and women. It's time we stand up and fight for the human rights Black men and women deserve!!!!"

-Joshua, 23, Trinidad and Tobago
June 5, 2020

"To the non-black people in my life watching from the sidelines: Look into your character and see if there's anything in there of use to help others.

And if there isn't anything there, if all you can do is look at yourself and say, I don't have it in me to be selfless at this time due to my beliefs and the content of my character, then please leave me alone. Leave your Black brothers and sisters alone. And I will pray that you are able to live beyond yourself one day."

-Morgan, 22, Boston, MA
June 6, 2020

why Democracy means, everybody but me."
-Langston Hughes

"I know everyone has been on edge these last few days, and these are very scary times. I believe the killing of George Floyd just opened everyone's eyes and now not all of us but most of us are speaking up about this unjust behavior that has been going on for years honestly. I think it's important that days like this we remain focused on what we really want and that's a just justice system. We all know there are bad apples everywhere, and every group has its bad apples but the consequences and the punishments for these crimes committed should be the same universally.

It should be the same despite your race, social economic class, resources and I think it's when you favor one race or you're more lenient towards another race that those people feel like they can get away with more and they continue to do things over and over again because at the end of the day they know they're only going to get a slap on the wrist and that's exactly what needs to end."

-Stephanie, 23, Queens, New York
June 7, 2020

"I come from a country with a lot of racism and separation despite us having such a diverse population. Moving to America brought racism into a whole new light for me. There is still colorism and anti-blackness present in POC groups, however there is a certain solidarity between the minority groups here.

This is especially true in New York City, a place where we watch each other's back and lend a hand when we can. Police brutality is just one drop in the ocean of systematic oppression in America against its Black citizens. We're not that far removed from Segregation and Jim Crowe, people alive today still remember those evils.

Thus, it must be heart breaking for them to see it still happening. American leaders, we're tired of all of you sitting idly by with your hands in your pocket. We don't want more Black men and women as hashtags, we want proper legislation that can finally put

an end to this cruel and brutal system that has

abused Black people in this country for hundreds of years.

-Shevin, 25, New York City
June 8, 2020

"With everything going on right now it's been difficult to truly express how I feel. I know I am angered, sad, frustrated, and confused but there's so much more, it's hard to put into words. I am sickened to see how deeply rooted racism, dis- crimination, and hypocrisy is within our country, but the ignorance and lack of compassion by a large portion of the population is truly frightening. To add to that, seeing racism and discrimination circulate within my own community against another minority group is just appalling.

My family is from Bangladesh, but I lived most of my life in Brooklyn, and not around many other Bangladeshi or South Asians for that matter. So, I won't speak against all South Asians, but I can say that as I got older, I started to notice the ignorance they brought with them from the old country. Colorism is a big issue in Bangladesh such that beauty is equated to a lighter skin tone, and you see this in the countless skin bleaching or complexion brightening cream ad campaigns.

This issue of colorism has undoubtedly turned to racism and discrimination within the community. I hear some of my fellow Bangladeshi Americans make derogatory comments about Black people yet they're oblivious to the Civil Rights movement that paved the way for South Asians to immigrate to America in the first place.

Many of them come to America to get away from poverty in Bangladesh and in search of a better life for their family but still believe in a false ideology that in order to do so you must appease to the white powers.

If there's anything that they should take away from what's going on now is that white suprema- cists don't care for us either, no matter how hard you try to appease them. It's up to our generation to question and fight our parents and grandparents on whatever ignorant ideologies they may still cling to, and to teach our kids what's right so that this cycle of injustice may finally come to an end."

-Aynul, 21, Queens, New York
June 11, 2020

Black Lives Matter Protests: Philadelphia
Photo by Caleb Johnson

"With everything that's been happening, I've been thinking more about racism in my community. My family comes from the Dominican Republic, where a vast majority of the population is mixed between Black (descendants of the West African Slaves) and White (descendants of the Spanish, French, etc. colonizers)—I happen to be a part of this mix too.

The unfortunate truth however is that many of these Dominicans often deny their blackness and prefer to believe that they are 'blanco oscuro' (dark white) or 'indiecito' (literally meaning Indian/Indigenous- like but is used to reference to tan skin). Race in my community often seems so difficult to discuss because, I've seen how people will go to concerning lengths to 'erase' their blackness with fairness creams and skin bleaching treatments- literally look at Sammy Sousa. And I've seen how people look at my natural hair and called it 'pelo malo' (bad hair) when it's curly, to then shower it with blessings and praises when it's pin straight, after a high heat two-hour Dominican blow out.

But as much as so many Dominicans want to cling to whiteness, I've seen how people look at me for having lighter skin. I remember some time ago when I was on the island and a young boy threw his trash at my feet as I passed him by. I remember the feeling of eyes on me—staring me down, and faces looking back at me in surprise when I spoke Spanish aloud.

If it feels like there's a dissonance here, it's because there is. I love who I am and where my family comes from but, I can't pretend that the Dominican government hasn't made things impossible for the Haitians, for being a reminder of our own blackness. I can't pretend that I haven't heard relatives hope that my cousins and I marry a white man, or a light skinned Dominican. And I can't pretend I haven't had to remind my own family of its own heritage from time to time...because if I didn't? I'd be adding to the problem instead of trying to help fix it. It's about time we had those uncomfortable conversations, it's been long overdue."

-Emely, 21, New York
June 10, 2020

Black Lives Matter Protests: Washington DC

"The minority community is the only reason the United States of America is still standing today. This nation was built on the backs of Black, Brown, and minority people, yet still within it there is a system of discrimination used to keep these very creators under the control of white supremacist. It actually blows my mind that ending racism is so controversial. We are simply asking others to treat all human beings as they would like to be treated.

There were many things that the US educational system failed to teach our young children regarding different minority cultures and the TRUTH behind the American system which is FAR from justice and liberty for all. Though one thing I vividly remember hearing is "treat others as you would like to be treated". They have raped, beaten, pillaged, murdered our minority communities, and laughed in our face about it.

For years we have been abused by the system, though when we retaliate this behavior through riots, fires, protesting for our rights, and fight for our place in the very nation we built as minority human beings we are still wrong. This is how we have been treated for generations though still we are in the wrong.

The white community has never been peaceful when demanding peace. It is time we stand together to finally put white supremacy and racism to an end. If we allow this to affect further generations, we have failed our ancestors, if we let this continue, we are telling our ancestors their rights never mattered and neither do ours or our future children.

All groups must stand together to defeat the plague of racism that affects every single minority in every single part of this vast world. Together we are the strongest. It's time for people to start fighting for something bigger than themselves."

-Cameron, 19, Farmingville
June 11, 2020

When I was about 10 years old, I would hang out with my neighbors, and they'd come over to my house all the time. My grandfather lived with us, and he'd tell my mom that he didn't want me hanging out with one of my friends because his skin was dark.

That's still crazy to me because it's not like we're white. We're all Dominican. And my friend that he was talking about was also Dominican. He was just darker than most of the people in my family. I never understood it. We all come from the same place. Why do my people reject those of darker skin tones? Why do people of darker skin tones reject their blackness? Do they not understand our history?

How come 80 years ago our dictator, Rafael Trujillo, indiscriminately massacred anywhere between 9,000 and 20,000 Haitians living in the Dominican Republic in 1937 in what is known as the Parsley Massacre.

Black and Latino people have constantly been told that we should just forget about the past and move on. But how can we move on so easily? Black people were subject to 400 years of slavery and then segregation and systemic racism.

People of Color (POC) were subject to redlining, stuck in neighborhoods that they wanted to move out of but couldn't. Redlining blocked entire black and Latino neighborhoods from access to private and public investments. Because of this, POC get rejected for bank loans more commonly than white people.

Why does implicit bias play a part when POC want to apply for a job?

Why does the US invest more money in the prison system than they do on educating children?

Why is there such a huge gap in wealth?

Black people and POC made this country what it is today. White people have had a 400-year head start on building generational wealth and too many times have I heard that POC need to "stop being lazy" and "have to deal with it because life isn't fair." People need to recognize their privilege. Systematic racism exists and the people who say otherwise (like National Security Advisor, Robert O'Brien) are ignorant to the fact.

And lastly, why does saying "Black Lives Matter" bother people so much. Asking for fucking equality bothers you so much?"

-Edison, 22, New York
June 11, 2020

"I saw a video the other day of a white social media influencer in the middle of a protest. She was wearing a fancy black dress and holding a "Black Lives Matter" sign. She was posing in the middle of the street among protesters while someone was taking her picture from different angles. I was at a loss for words after watching that. All around me I see ways in which mere sentimentality and complacency have been decorated as meaningful action.

In a lot of ways, I am hurt that the movement has become a 'trend' for many. I do see the ways in which meaningful allies have rallied in the past couple of weeks, but the video I saw speaks volumes on how the gravity of this movement can be so easily overlooked.

As the timeline starts to get back to the mundane, let us not forget what these past couple of weeks have shown us and let us not allow anyone else to forget either."

-Ariana, 20, New York
June 11, 2020

The last few weeks have been overwhelming to say the least. Feeling sad, angry, moved, motivated, and drained all at once. Sad because of the countless wrongful deaths in the black community. Angry at the police and the government (especially the president).

Moved by the stories of others and the solidarity being shown. Motivated to take action and make a real change. Drained because it's a lot. It's uncomfortable. But that's the point. America has never been great. It was built by slave labor on stolen land. It's inherently racist. Yet, there are hundreds of thousands of people going out to protest every day, risking their lives to a deadly virus and police brutality. And so, there's hope. Hope for real systematic change.

Hope for an America that we can actually be proud of. Hope that we can eradicate racism. Until then, get comfortable being uncomfortable and feeling overwhelmed. Because until "All Lives Matter" includes Black lives, there is more work to be done."

-Demi, 23, Leeds, England
June 13, 2020

Similar to many African immigrants in the US, I come from a country where Black people are the majority. I have never been exposed to racism or any form of discrimination until I came to this country. Living in the South Bronx and having to travel to Manhattan for essentials such as medical care quickly showed me the disparities in the quality of life between Black and White people in this country.

As my years living here increased and I started engaging with institutions such as universities and firms, while taking courses and reading books on the lasting legacies of slavery in the US, it became clear to me that racism in the United States is not just an individual's prejudice or bias, but it is embedded in the systems, laws, and policies that in return oppress all Black people living here.

"My humanity is bound up in yours, for we only can be human together."

-Desmond Tutu

Since the start of the current protests and discourse around race that has been fueled by the gruesome killing of George Floyd, I had to engage myself in honest reflections on the role I play in this unjust society. For me and the many African immigrants living here, slavery did not rob us of having the opportunity to know the origins of our ancestors, be well versed in our native languages, cultures, and traditions, and have a sense of belonging somewhere. As a result, for some, this might provide the shameful impression that as long as we have the privilege to differentiate ourselves from African Americans who have for a long time been fighting these oppressive systems.

This impression is not only untrue, but it is also very dangerous. The systemic racism in this country unequivocally disadvantages and puts the lives of all Black people regardless of origin, prestige, or belief, at constant risk. Therefore, I will continue to check myself and let my communities know that this fight for justice, freedom, and equity is a fight that we must all be engaged in at all levels.

-AjiFanta, 23, Bronx NY
June 14, 2020

"In the US black people are being targeted, mistreated, undervalued and it started 400+ years ago. Every year since I was born, black injustice was in the headlines in some type of fashion but in my lifetime the person who started the conversation for change that I truly noticed and caught my attention was Colin Kaepernick. This race war has been going on for so long and now with social media and camera-phones, it's being shown vividly, making everyone aware of the dire need for change. Colin Kap was the young black man that used his athlete platform to honor those who had fallen in the name of social injustice. He was the spark that started it all.

As a black female athlete, I feel very strongly about using my platform for education and communication. I believe a lot of people don't know to the full extent what has been happening in the US. Seeing it myself, it's hurtful. I had to take a couple days off mentally from social media because I was crying and hurting seeing some of the violence in certain protests, seeing white people protest against the Black Lives Matter movement right near me in NY & seeing the police brutality. It's overwhelming and its honestly hard to believe that it's still happening. Watching Movies like Hidden Figures, The 13th, The Help, Malcolm X, it opens your eyes to the suffering. But in those moments where I broke down, I thought about all those who had fought for my voice and my freedoms. All those who have come before me and allowed me to live this life; They didn't stop fighting and neither will I.

Patrick Mahomes using his platform to drive change saying, "We need to be the role models", is absolutely right. Everyone says athletes are role models, so we need to use our platforms to promote positive change, we need to show our fans what we, as black athletes, go through and that we stand for All Black Lives. I'm hoping that we are the generation that ends this Race War. We are calling out people and companies to see where they stand, and they are showing their true colors.

We athletes are strong, dedicated, and resilient and we need to stand together and use our voices and our work ethic to create equality! We don't quit until we win, we won't quit until All Black Lives Matter..."

-Priscilla, 31, Antigua and Barbuda
June 14, 2020

"When I saw the death of Ahmaud Arbery, I was so shocked. A man running in broad daylight just minding his business could be followed and shot by two civilians. The video sparked something in me that I know was also sparked within the community of Black people. We didn't want the shooters to get away with such a heinous and hateful crime. I signed many petitions to make sure justice was received for him and his family. Just as the attention on Ahmaud was fading, another heinous and hateful act was committed on George Floyd and this time by 4 police officers. For 8 minutes and 46 seconds a man was violated by the system that was meant to serve and protect. I haven't understood the reason for backlash whenever we say that Black Lives Matter.

If I were any other race and saw both of those videos and the countless other names of people that haven't received any justice, I would have compassion because nobody deserves to be murdered in such a fashion. It is shame that there are people opposing the Black Lives Matter Movement. People saying that if we take away cops that we would live in chaos.

But how can they continue to be praised when there are so many flaws in the system. My only hope is that we don't stop pressuring the government, protesting in the streets, and promoting black business. Even when they give us a quick fix or a "chokehold ban" that is not the reform we are asking for. Enough is enough, We are fed up, this is the greatest time to be loud and proactive. We must push for a radical change."

-Steve, 21, New York
June 15, 2020

LIVING IN TWO A

INSPIRED BY THE CAPITAL RIOTS ON JANUARY 6, 2021, WHERE WHITE RIOTERS STORMED THE CAPITOL FORCING CONGRESSMEN AND WOMEN TO TAKE REFUGE.

SPURRED BY RHETORIC OF A STOLEN ELECTION FROM PRESIDENT TRUMP, THE SCENES FROM THAT DAY WERE HORRIFIC AND SHOWED THE UGLINESS KNOWN BEHIND THE VEIL.

THIS IS FINAL PART OF THE 'LIVING IN TWO AMERICAS' SERIES.

January 10, 2021,
New York

Growing up in Guyana, my mother would always say to me: "When yuh buy ah dutty calico yuh gat fuh wear am till it tear." It's a Guyanese proverb that means: "When you make a decision you must be prepared to live with the consequences." I've tried to live my life by this saying, but in the wake of the domestic terrorist attack on the US Capitol by white supremacists, this proverb has taken on new meaning. Since Wednesday, I've heard the question "How did we get here?" asked on social media, on news outlets by TV personalities. It's a serious question. One that demands introspection from all Americans. But if you're a black person in America, that question has been reverberating in your head for years. And you already know the answers.

Over the last four years, the phrase 'Make America Great Again' (MAGA) has been repeated by President Trump, republicans, and his supporters. It's a phrase that's been the foundation of his racist, xenophobic, and white supremacist platform. It's also a phrase that has become emblematic of the racism and white supremacy that has become increasingly visible in society. When white Americans voted for Trump in 2016, they knew what they were getting. While the argument persists that no one could predict everything he would do in the four years of his presidency, the warning signs were still there. And many did predict it. During his presidency, some of us watched in horror as the U.S transitioned to being great again. He's politicized the army, refused to show his tax returns, used his office to bolster his businesses, abused appointment power, launched an attack on the press, and of course refused to denounce white supremacists.

How could you watch the events of the last four years, yet still vote for Trump in 2020? How could you still vote for someone who has launched assaults on democracy and press freedom, peddled fear, racism, and exclusion in addition to everything else you've seen? How could you still vote for Trump? How could you claim your position as a white ally to the Black community and BLM and still vote for a man like Trump? To do so only illuminates white privilege. What your choice discloses is that despite seeing the evil, and injustices, there are some things you are willing to excuse to still vote for him. Why? Because the issues don't affect you.

It's been very frustrating to hear the white people who voted for Trump say they didn't vote for this (if they say anything at all). To watch the lack of accountability, the lack of introspection, and the privilege on display in many ways goes beyond frustrating to disgusting. There must be accountability. Living in an America where you're not confronted by the issues, the injustices, and the failings of the system, brings with it a complacency. An aunt of mine said something to me on Thursday that described the anger I was feeling: White Silence is compliance.

MERICAS PT. 2

Written by Daniel Haynes

It doesn't matter that you say you support Black Lives Matter, share the posts on social media when it's trendy, or even have a conversation with your black friends about how wrong everything is especially if you voted for trump in 2020. You have contributed to what this country has become. For years Black people have said there's an issue, for years we've expressed the fear that we have as we've watched our people die. We've cried about it, screamed about it, protested it but have had to swallow that pain and live in an America that was never designed for us.

It doesn't matter that you say you support Black Lives Matter, share the posts on social media when it's trendy, or even have a conversation with your black friends about how wrong everything is especially if you voted for Trump in 2020. You have contributed to what this country has become. For years Black people have said there's an issue, for years we've expressed the fear that we have as we've watched our people die. We've cried about it, screamed about it, protested it but have had to swallow that pain and live in an America that was never designed for us.

Photo by Luana Seu

If you're one of the 75 million votes Trump received, you enabled Trump's rhetoric. The claims of voter fraud, claims of a stolen election, calls to storm the Capitol. How you ask? The answer is in the proverb I mentioned earlier: every decision has a consequence that you need to live by. This is a moment to sit and process that. If you're white and you haven't also called out incidents of racism, of privilege, of systemic failings then you are also part of the problem. You can't call yourself an ally if you address the issue and share the posts when it's convenient to you. There's another Guyanese proverb I grew up hearing: "Cat a ketch rat, but he a teef he massa fish". It means good and evil can come from the source.

I know it's difficult to have a conversation about race every day, and it is exhausting. White Americans and whites in America have that choice. For blacks in America, it isn't a conversation, it's a lived experience every day of our lives. The same fear that Nancy Pelosi and other white congressmen and women felt when white supremacists were searching for them, looking to kill them, and marching with Confederate flags is the same fear us black and brown people live with every day.

Welcome to our America.

MY AMERI...

"The first thing they teach you in a high school civics class is the Bill of Rights otherwise known as the first 10 amendments to the Constitution of the United States. The first of those rights is the Freedom of religion, speech, press, assembly, and petition. With this country being founded on the principles of protest and revolution, this initial right is often lost in the shuffle of others, seen as a sign of ungratefulness to those who are supposed to uphold "freedom".

Growing up in conservative military communities throughout the United States, I became very aware about the rights of US citizens at an early age, particularly the right to bear arms. Yet, I was not encouraged to exercise my other rights, especially those of the first amendment as I grew to understand how the military did not have these rights themselves. As a young queer woman of color, who also happened to be a first generation American, I began to question more and more the supposed rights that I had, surrounded by an extremely patriarchal and at times misogynistic lens. With political unrest growing more and more as I headed into my adult years, stepping further away from patriarchal environments, I fully began to utilize my duty to challenge the government I saw as unfit.

In 2017, I joined the Women's March in Savannah, GA following the inauguration of "He who must not be named". Feeling extremely fearful, I was met with much support from both peers and professors alike. Never had I felt such hope and community in demanding autonomy over women's bodies and minds alike. After expressing my experiences with my innocent optimism, I received shame and negativity from my family. How dare I challenge a country that had given me so much when other countries have nothing! "What will people say?" Flash forward to 2020 and that shame and fear loomed over me as I desired both justice along with peace. I had never felt so childlike and small as I weakly responded to triggering violence.

On May 25th, 2020, the day of George Floyd's murder, and the subsequent surge of Black Lives Matter protests I was ironically in a conservative town in Florida watching everything unfold on social media. My pain over the situation turned into hope as I saw people of all colors 'take to the streets' in solidarity online.

Just as quickly as I had hope, did it turn into pure horror once I saw the response of police and governments alike. With more and more blood spilling, it seemed that the so called "first amendment right of assembly" were nothing more than words on a page. My insecurities of shame and fear of harm as I wanted to stand against injustice rose within me. As much as I wanted to be physically present, I feared for my own life, as I considered how my own family would not support me nor protect me from a government, they were loyal to. At the same time, I feared for my friends who had more courage than I had at the time as they took to the streets.

Fear is an emotion I have felt immensely throughout these past 2 years. The fear of losing personal autonomy, and of never having true prosperity for all. Living in the shadows is nothing new for me as a queer woman; but I, along with many others find ourselves forced to support from behind the scenes out of fear of physical safety. This has only gotten worse with the overturn of Roe v Wade. More and more, people who oppose white Christian patriarchal values are pushed to live in the shadows as America turns into the thing it not only hates the most, but also killed many in the Middle East for-a religious nation that turns the idea of "God" into law. It truly makes me wonder if fear itself was the true goal.

In a high school civics course, you learn about the laws of this country, and the history of those laws. What they don't explicitly teach you is how those laws were initially created for white men who owned land. They don't teach you the nuances of the Constitution and how WE as people of color were never supposed to benefit from such laws. Many have been silenced by fear but what we don't realize is that as long as a document such as the Constitution does not change, they will continue to betray us."

-Natalie. D, 24, New York
July 7, 2022

Roe v Wade Protests Detroit
Photos by Lamar Price

Black Lives Matter
Photos by

Protests: Philadelphia.
Caleb Johnson

CHAPTER

FOUR

Reflections, Hopes & Dreams

Black Lives Matter Protests: Washington DC

"It has been a rough week seeing the unjust killing of George Floyd, and the protests that are happening globally are necessary, and it shows how hurt we as a people are. The Black and minority communities have dealt with racism, police brutality, and we as a people have not been seen as equals for hundreds of years. We've seen history repeat itself again and again and we have had enough!

Now is the time to fight for change so that we can have a future where we don't see unjust killings by the police, as well as a future where people of color are seen as an equal. In fighting for change and a better future we not only need to unite as a people, but also put our faith and trust in God to guide us through these times."

-Drew, 22, New Jersey
June 1, 2020

Just because he was a Black man

G one from this world forever, just because he was a Black man

E xample of the all too frequent atrocities occurring, just because he was a Black man

O stracised by society, just because he was a black man

R acially profiled, just because he was a Black man

G iven no chance to defend himself, just because he was a Black man

E nded up yet another sad statistic of racial violence, just because he was a Black man

F ramed his entire life by his race, just because he was a Black man

L oved by many but hated by more, just because he was a Black man

O ther men commit far worse crimes but he died for his, just because he was a Black man

Y earning to breathe but dying of asphyxiation, just because he was a Black man

D ead for a minor misdemeanour, just because he was a Black man

May George Floyd be the instigator for the imperative and massive paradigm shift in perception, treatment and acceptability that needs to take place so that his life was not lost in vain, just because he was a Black man.

-Philippa, 53, Nassau The Bahamas
June 3, 2020

"How do I feel right now? I'm tired... Never in my lifetime could I have dreamed the world existing in the state it is right now. People trying to survive a pan- demic and others still going through the struggle of what it means to be Black in this country. The fact that there's even a conversation going on about where Black lives matter... whether I deserve to live or not. What has always seemed like common sense to me, is lost amongst the white population. So, you've asked me what I think. I think God has granted my generation the strength to tear our- selves out of this oppression and create a safe tomorrow."

-Sondrea, 21, Albany, NY
June 10, 2020

"Unfortunately, I've always been privy to racism, whether in word or deed. How- ever, as a student athlete in South Carolina I have not experienced any racist acts personally, but I am not numb to the truth about racist acts towards minorities in America. My understanding of racism in America stemmed from a video I saw with a white woman spitting racial slurs at a Mexican woman on the subway. it was a demonstration of the "white privilege" I've so often heard of. So, experiences like that make me believe that the current ongoing protests promoting the #BlackLivesMatter movement are necessary.

I personally believe that this movement is asking for the mere minimum, and the fact that it is being met with so much resistance from the pressing forces, says a lot about who persons in America believe should be treated equally."

-Arinze, 24, Columbia, SC
June 11, 2020

"As a Black man in today's society, I am disheartened and angry about the climate of black lives in America. A con- tinuation of lives of innocent Black men

and women have been cut short due to the reckless behavior of cops, but a selfish system in racism. To know the lives of Black people is at risk on a daily basis scares me because we have so much to offer, but the system wants to shut us down. Life at times feels like a constant nightmare and I'm just hoping to wake up.

I feel disheartened, but I am hopeful. Just to know that many Black people around the United States and around the globe, in person or on social media have risen to the occasion. Every protest, every post, every like, and retweet show we are a family that will fight for one another. We have really pulled together as one. We have lifted up our voices once again and we have been heard.

We have shook the world with our unity in the stance against injustice. We are demanding change for the better so the ones that come after us can have a life worth living. Each and every Black person that stood up not only demonstrated that their lives matter, but we are excellent, we are light, we are love, and we are worth living. We are our brother's and sister's keeper.

This continues to make me hopeful. We cannot be killed off. I'm praying and hoping for more change and more justice. I pray that the pain of many families is healed. I pray the people in higher positions bring justice to the lives that have been lost. We are worthy, beloved, and needed. I won't stop shouting until I truly feel this way."

-Marvelous, 22, Boston MA
June 12, 2020

"These disturbing times have affected me in many unexpected ways. I have felt grief, sadness, stress, anger, and many other weird in-between emotions that I've never felt before.

I feel exhausted at the end of each day despite the fact that I haven't moved around much during the day (hence also living through a pandemic that has us all at home). But very thankfully, my main joy has been that this trouble is strengthening my trust in God.

It's been a very psychosomatic experience—seeing my fellow Black people struggling makes me physically tired each day. Yet, in the midst of it, I have peace knowing that the fallen nature of this world is not the end; this world is hopeless, but I don't have to be.

And that's because in the midst of fighting for justice, I know that our Creator has already achieved true justice and it will be revealed and enjoyed by His children in the future, when the earth is no more."

-Alexandria, 21, PG County, Maryland
June 12, 2020

"I'm reassessing my belief in hope. I find it very easy to feel cynical, like this time will pass, people will tire, and the energy activating this moment of change will subside. The Bible says that even "youths grow weary". I feel like a weary youth, a witness, who has cried out around injustice for so long. But I've decided that I will not give into cynicism completely. I choose instead to be proactively hopeful.

I believe that when the new converts against injustice grow weary, that is, those who are only now been galvanized to march, are tired, it will be the work of those of us who have been consistent to continue the fight for justice. We the consistent, are the artists, the activists, the advocates. So, I take this time of mainstream collective energy as a moment for me to rest, replenish and reinforce.

For when they grow weary, it will be my time again to fight."

-Liz, 29, New York
June 15, 2020

"It's important for us to also understand that the phrase 'Black Lives Matter' simply refers to the notion that there's a specific vulnerability for African Americans that needs to be addressed. It's not meant to suggest that other lives don't matter. It's to suggest that other folks aren't experiencing this particular vulnerability."

-Barack Obama

"Throughout the past few weeks, I find myself staring at the calendar more often than what I normally would have. Birthdays, doctor appointments, and work schedules have no longer been part of my 'typical' events to check the calendar. Instead, I find myself dissecting this apocalyptic year into its grueling months.

Starting with January—a month marked by a major international political crisis, Australia's uncontrolled bush fires, and the loss of nine lives by a helicopter crash in California. The year begins to mourn.

February—the world is busy with political, social, and economic chaos as the death of Ahmaud Arbery becomes muzzled in the midst of other 'news' that the media chooses to present instead.

March—the cycle continues. Overwhelmed by COVID-19 updates and disarray, the shooting of Breonna Taylor is also hushed. April and May come along, and although the limits of social distancing have completely changed our ways of life, we became more connected than ever through the power of social media.

I kept seeing George Floyd's name all over my feed and eventually stumbled upon the video depicting his final moments of life. Just hours following his death, waves of videos and stories of other Black individuals including those I mentioned earlier, started flooding our feeds.

I cried myself to sleep that night. It's one thing to know that racism exists, but it's another thing to experience it and be aware of how embedded it actually is in present-day life.

I keep wondering about the millions of other dates in which other Black individuals have cried out for help, only to be silenced by the corrupt system controlling our news and departments of 'justice.'

How many days, months, perhaps even centuries will this racism pandemic continue to spread, mutate, and camouflage itself into ways that it can often go undetected and silently kill its victims? I pray that our generation continues to be vocal and fearless in this world controlled by those who will do anything to silence us."

-Pamela, 20, Bay Shore, NY
June 15, 2020

Black Lives Matter Protests in Detroit
Photos by Lamar Price

"MY STORY O

"So much is going on in our world but yet I'm also thinking about the personal milestone for my family and continue to mourn the loss of my father. I have to juggle my emotions and my pain. I have to choose what I share because in this moment, every word, post, comment or thought matters.

This month marks 35 years since my father was shot to death while he was at work at a gas station. And this month alone we have lost several African Americans to the hands of racist vigilantes and cops. One shot to the chest killed my father instantly, and in the blink of an eye my immigrant family was forever shattered. A Nigerian family of 6 became 5, a wife became a widow and a single parent, and 4 children were instantly fatherless. We came to America in search of the American dream, which some- how turned into a nightmare. We left Nigeria because my father got accepted to Liverpool University in London, and we left London because he was accepted into the master's program at NYU. We were here on his student visa and now deportation was a very real threat for us because of the careless actions of two people.

The night of my father's murder, it was only three weeks after my family moved from NY to MD, so we were still adjusting. I remember my siblings and I received a phone call late that evening from my cousins to tell us my father was dead. Naturally we didn't believe it, because it was just an impossible thing to wrap our young brains around. I was 9 years old, and my siblings were 13, 11, and 5. We waited for my mother to come home (no cell phones in 1985), and as she walked in the door with my father's blood on her clothes, it all started to sink in. She was there with my father at the gas station waiting for him to close up shop so they could walk home together. But two teenagers walked in with ski masks on, pointed the gun at him and asked for the money in the register. He gave it to them, and they still shot him. My mother was in the back and heard the gun shot and ran out. They shot at her too but missed and ran off. My father died in her arms.

I often think of how we could have been orphans in that moment and God only knows what my life would have become!! I can't even remember how she told us the tragic news, but I remember just going numb. And since then, so much of my childhood is a blur. Perhaps the defense mechanism of a young child that experiences trauma. In hindsight, I see very clearly the damage my father's death has on me... still till this day! Trauma and PTSD is real!!

I've rarely, if ever shared the full details of my father or brother's murder. But I share tonight my father's, to give you perspective on trauma. When someone is tragically taken from your life, it leaves a scar that can never heal. When cops kill our Kings and Queens, their families are traumatized. So is all the Black American community because we know it could be one of us. It could be our grandfathers, our

F TRAUMA..."

fathers, our brothers, our cousins, our uncles, our nephews, our grandmothers, our mothers, our aunts, our sisters, our nieces. This is no way to live life. We hold our breath when a loved one is delayed coming home and jump when the phone rings praying it's not bad news. I didn't grow up with social media and don't know how traumatic it must be to watch videos on social media of your loved ones dying and to watch the news reports showing that video over and over. But right now, it's all we have—to show proof of our killings—and even that isn't enough for people to see the inhuman injustice.

I remember being traumatized in the court room because during the trial is when you see it all. The crime scene images, and the murderers' testimonies. You hear the lawyers lying and doing everything in their power to get the perps off. And then you wait for the "jury of your peers" to determine guilt. But when you are Black in America, the deck is stacked against you. The jury is not of your peers. The system works against you and your murderers walk free. We were fortunate that the murderers of both my father and brother were caught and the majority of them are serving a life sentence or served some time and are released now (yea that sucks too, knowing that they are out free...so imagine getting no justice at all??? But what I often wonder is this. If my families' murderers weren't Black, would they have gotten off? We have seen time and time again a system that makes Black men and women pay for their crimes but gives a slap on the wrist to white people. All we want is an equal system that says if you commit the crime, you do the time. These cops and vigilantes should not go free when someone lost their lives.

One thing I know firsthand is the pain that comes with saying goodbye to your loved ones and NEVER seeing them again. That is what every Black person experiences every day. We wonder if this will be the day that we die by the hands of a racist vigilante or a racist cop! Black mothers live in fear. Black sisters live in fear. We cry real tears for people we have never met because we have empathy and feel their pain. This is a human fight. And everyone needs to decide which side they are on. The world is watching, we are watching, I am watching. I miss my father and brother every day. Part of me sometimes feels peace that they are not here to continue to experience the racism and risks of being black in America. But this little girl, would give anything to have her father back. And everything I do is for Kingsley, my father, my original protector, and my king.

RIP dad! I love you and all our fallen soldiers!"

-Joy, 40s, Washington DC
June 15, 2020

Rest In
George Floyd
Cedrick Chatman
Anthony Harris
Russell Smith
Fred Bradford
Marlon Brown
Bill Jackson
George Harvey
Allen Desdunes
William Taylor
Jeffery Ragland
Yvette Smith
Eric Ricks
Brian Pickett
Leslie Sapp III
Yolanda Thomas
Charles Baker
Jermain Darden
Keoshia Hill
Antonio Johnson
Dainell Simmons
Jermain McBean
Marlon Horton
Abdul Kamal
Jordan Baker
Gone

Black Lives Matter Protests:

Washington DC

GEORGE FLOYD: T

"Almost two years later exactly, I am here providing a perspective on events that have exposed the deep divide between Americans that challenge the core values of our nation.

Since the murder of Mr. Floyd, a single former police officer has been stripped of his authority and sentenced to 20 years in prison for violating the civil rights of a citizen. In my opinion, this is excellent news, however, the objectives that the African American community want to accomplish and the dignity that we as a people deserve have not yet been met.

Institutionalized injustice still has a hold on the American system. Malpractice can be seen in a variety of spaces, such as police encounters, home buying, appraisals, the historic residue of red lining, banking, education, and recently, the ability to participate in the democratic process as a citizen during our election period. And as a result, we see young men and women being harmed and killed in common spaces. What is done on the level of legislation, and economics, will show itself in day-to-day encounters. These former officers took George's life because at some level they believed that their actions were affirmed by the authority of Minnesota. How we treat people at every encounter provides a sense of what the minimum level of decency is required when interacting with that community.

Across the country, we understand that there are some people that see that level of decency toward black people in the United States as incredibly low. We as a community are in real and present danger that is often not originating from news like two years ago. Instead? A deeply held opinion about an American community that shows itself in events like that one.

The majority are tired of working towards a future that keeps our peers and children safe to the same level that other citizens get to enjoy. As a person who has studied media, and communication, and is currently pursuing their Masters' degree in similar subjects, there are some practices, and lessons that I believe can be useful in situations like Mr. Floyd's murder. They also offer a holistic improvement to this American community. The values, and attitudes that we can strengthen have the possibility to change how we see ourselves, and therefore improve the story that we tell each other and the world.

Alexa

Developing a stronger sense of the values that make a community.

We must work together. Family is the first building block of any group. It is what we first interact with and learn from. Our core beliefs are founded there among them. Many of our children across the nation are products of single-parent homes for a variety of reasons, ultimately leaving youth at a disadvantage. We must reinforce what it means to treat one another well, what it means to not just be a brother and son but also a husband, and the same aspects for women. Emphasizing these characteristics at a familial level in my belief will inspire the creation of whole families with both parents and provide a more stable possibility for youth throughout America.

Marriages create a better chance to build wealth. In a survey created by YouGov, readers understand that there is a growing sentiment that "More adults generally agreed being legally married is less important than having a "personal sense of

WO YEARS LATER

Written by Alexander Coger-Bonet

July 8, 2022

nder Coger-Bonet

commitment to your partner." It is a shortsighted approach to the future. By legally marrying both parties, people are likely to increase their earnings via cultural opportunities, tax benefits, a safer retirement, and a dedicated system in place to pass those resources down to children.

Emphasize education and network.

You can never take away what a person knows. Children are the backbone of America; it only makes sense to provide them the best you can offer them and surround them with those who are interested in doing the same. With education comes the chance to develop wealth and philanthropy. Giving back can be an investment of a person's time; creating intern opportunities at black businesses, working with youth post-graduation, or strengthening the institutions that helped you achieve what you currently have are all options. I am a product of what I suggest.

The Midnight Golf Program is designed to work with high school seniors in the Southeast area of Michigan to determine college application, personal finance, scholarship submission, and the game of golf which is a common way to network and pitch ideas in corporate work settings. The Emma Bowen Foundation was created to place minority people in the media industry which is currently dominated by white people. Without organizations like these, I would have never made the choice to attend college where I do now or have my first internship with a major company. These actions can be repeated by others and deserve more investment to push more young people further.

There is no guarantee that if George Floyd or the hundreds of other people who have lost their lives were products of the messages that I believe in, they would have survived. Thinking of this situation for the past two years, the only recurring idea is what has been written above. Staying together, and striving for the best we can achieve, is a catalyst for a better chance to win the battle for equity every time something like this happens. Up to the point where it is won, we can then see ourselves in every aspect of the American dream where the values of this country are just as meaningful to us as every other citizen.

We are in a unique time where if we focus on those two goals, we can bring our own chair to the national conversation, stop another

Floyd situation and bridge the divide in this country.

"THIS IS AMERICA..."

Written by Anthony Martin

July 9, 2022

Daniel asked for an updated reflection on what's transpired in this country since 2020. Two years later and nothing's changed. But honestly how can we expect it to when the system has always been like this? We just so happen to be living in the present version of this system.

Covid is still running rampant. We still value guns and the color blue more than our kids, and more than the colors Black and Brown. Our economy is plummeting, people are more divided politically than ever, and old white politicians are making decisions on our women's bodies. Our infrastructure and education systems are underfunded and need more aid. It's clear our healthcare system needs continual work. Social media has given platforms to those who promote hate, violence, racism, and bigotry.

This Is America.

It's funny because it's supposed to be "We The People" but the people really have no say. We vote and nothing changes. We petition and protest and nothing changes. We celebrate small victories that don't push the needle far enough for actual change. Because of this, we feel the need to place blame on one another. We point fingers at our brothers and sisters. We lack unity. Personally, I believe this is done purposely. How can we expect true change when we can't agree or come together on anything? As much as we can blame the government for our issues, we need to self-reflect and take a look at ourselves.

Collectively we need to do better.

As I get older, I find I have less hope in this country, and I am not "proud" to be an American. About a month ago, my friends and I were at a sporting event and didn't stand for the national anthem. You could feel the stares like hot daggers, but why should I stand for a flag that has never represented ALL the American people. Until the poor, the discriminated, the minority, the disabled, the disenfranchised, and the under- represented are seen and valued in this country, we will never make progress. These groups together make up the majority but need the most help.

What's interesting is, while all this takes place, you can still see the potential a country like this can have. It gives us a glimmer of hope. A unique melting pot of cultures, religions, and creeds. But just because something is good enough, doesn't mean we should strive to make it better. We need to be more compassionate, create new systems, new political structures, and implement new voices that represent the people of America. If we don't, it's only a matter of time before the pot boils over.

Anthony Martin. Photo by Daniel C. Haynes

“OUR LOST VOIC

"Something came over me when I was in the process of planning it all.

Organizing a protest was truly a way for me to cope with the pain of feeling such a disconnect with my own people. Moving out of the Bronx and coming into a community that was predominantly white during my teenage years did a number to my spirit and identity. It wasn't until George Floyd's video had surfaced on the Internet and I was met with that inner pain/loneliness of my own reality.

Many years of constantly coexisting with white people made me numb to their silence. I didn't realize how separate I felt from my own people and now that we're in the year 2022, I want to give thanks to George Floyd, Breonna Taylor, & Ahmaud Aubrey for waking me up to this in such a way that will forever be timeless. Their lives put me in a position to expand my understanding of what it means not only to be black but to be human.
If it wasn't for their stories being heard, I probably would've still been in a state of passiveness when it came to what it meant to be Black. I probably would've never come to the realization on how important unity was for me.

It was as if the anger and grief of 2020 was always there within me, (simmering below the surface) just waiting to come out. I believe that this was the universal lesson of it all. Not only as a community but also as a society we learned the importance of unity, support, and awareness. We discovered that we lack so much of these values and even worse, choose to apply these values under ignorant or biased views. We read and listened to the stories of all walks of life that have been affected by this cruel reality and it's just a beautiful thing to acknowledge how far we've come with these universal lessons.

Most of the BLM movement was being pushed by the youth. At a time that felt so unsafe, it was shocking to see that shift. The younger generation taking charge and spreading their leadership skills is something that can't be forgotten. I personally believe that this energy must always be maintained and consistent for the well-being of minorities and other worldly issues as well. We can now find interest on deeper issues as the young generation. The generation that has the power to be unapologetic, fast-paced, and creative all at once. What a time to be alive, where now this can all be incorporated for the greater good.

We must give thanks to these angels for touching our hearts in such a way that we had no choice but to be loud. I even look back and reflect on how traumatic the media was in the year 2020 with our phones constantly ringing to trauma porn. It all now feels like a band-aid, and with that being said, if you don't know pain how can you know love? Even though there is still much work to be done within a political standpoint when talking about race, it's time we show some grace to the younger generation that took time out of their days to work towards a Black Lives Matter movement. Look back at the process that was taken in order for our voices to be seen on the media-especially if you were living in a small town/ community and be proud of what you did to leave a mark.

Exercising leadership put us all in a position to see ourselves in such a helpful way. Most of the protesters were afraid to show up for this cause but knowing we were all going to have each other's back in a way that was felt across the entire nation, was enough to eliminate the fear and doubt. I truly believe that we went above and beyond, digging deep in to our own individual bravery.

ES..."

Written by Ange Musoni

Black Lives Matter Protests: New Jersey. Photo by Isaiah Gill

Personally, putting a protest together really made me see myself in a different light and at that time I needed that. I was able to see a small voice create a ripple affect. In a time when so many young people were battling mental illness, that was crucial. We all get the equal opportunity of having purpose within this life. Whether we know it or not, the lives lost always live on and carry purpose for the next lives to come. We are at a place now where we can sit and look back at this and vocalize our gratitude. I don't believe this was done enough during the last three years, and with so many changes happening to everyone in all aspects of life, it was easy for this to go over our heads.

In conclusion, I want to offer a space for gratitude to be shown amongst the lives lost. They deserve a thank you for putting such fire in our bellies to change for the better. They deserve a thank you for leaving a mark on our hearts and nation. Not everything within activism and human rights have all to do with anger and blame. There is always love and wanting to feel not alone that comes along with it too.

Be grateful for your Blackness & Black lives.

It will always count.

US

Photo by Luana Seu

NOTE FROM THE AUTHOR

While originally editing what would become this book in 2020, another heartbreaking story made the news. It was the story of Elijah McClain, another Black man killed by police. His last words also included the phrase "I can't breathe." He was killed at the age of 23 in the summer of 2019 while walking home from the grocery store. His crime? Being Black and wearing a ski-mask. The mask was to help with his social anxiety.

I was 23 years old in the summer of 2019, and when I wrote this a year later it was impossible to fight the tears, the anger, and the pain I felt. However, it was just another page in the chapter of the book that's called being Black in America.

A New York Times article on June 28, 2020, showed another 70 people said the now infamous phrase "I can't breathe", but still died in police custody.

Since the protests in 2020, America has lived through a lot. Gun control is still an issue facing us today, mass shootings continue to be as common as a summer shower, and the U.S. Supreme Court overturned Roe v Wade removing abortion rights for many away across the country.

In September of 2020, none of the three officers in the Breonna Taylor case were criminally charged with killing her. One officer was indicted for wanton endangerment for firing into a neighboring apartment on the night Breonna was killed. The maximum sentence for this charge is five years. The minimum? One.

The three officers who killed George Floyd were all found guilty in a Federal civil rights trial in April, 10 months after his vile murder. Derek Chauvin, the officer who kneeled on George Floyd's neck was found guilty on all three counts including second-degree unintentional murder, third-degree murder, and second-degree manslaughter. He became the first white Minnesota police officer to be convicted of murdering a black person.

In November of 2021, the City of Aurora, Colorado agreed a $15 million settlement with Elijah McClain's family for a civil rights lawsuit filed after his tragic death.

The three men who murdered Ahmaud Arbery were also found guilty of 'Hate crimes in connection with the pursuit and killing of Ahmaud Arbery' in February of 2022, signaling some semblance of progress. Father and son, Gregory, and Travis McMichael, were each sentenced to life imprisonment without the possibility of parole. Accomplice William "Roddie" Bryan was sentenced to life imprisonment with the possibility of parole.

However, since George Floyd's death and the promises of lawmakers, The Washington Post collected data that shows police have shot and killed 1,055 people nationwide in 2021, an increase from the 1,021 shootings in 2020. What percentage of those shootings were Black people?

27%

Twenty-seven percent of the people that were fatally shot in 2021 were Black people who account for only 13% of the US population according to non-profit group Mapping Police Violence. Mapping Police Violence tracks police shootings, and their statistic shows that Black people are twice as likely as white people to be shot and killed by police officers.

In June 2020, the pain, the fear, and the justified anger we the Black community carry with us daily was displayed. We still sit in your classrooms, walk your streets, ride the buses and the subway. We work beside you, eat in the same restaurants, and bleed the same. We do everything you do, except live a life that is free and equal. Except live in fear that our next moment could be our last.

In this book you have read the stories of Black people, you have seen our pain. You have read the stories of our allies and seen their commitment to fighting alongside us. You have read the calls to action, the calls for equality, and you've seen the reflections of hopes, dreams, and prayers. It is my hope that this book stands as a window, through which we see the time the world stood still and marched in support of **Black Lives everywhere**.

In the next pages you will find the curated stories of three Black men living their passions, walking in their purposes, and creating a lasting legacy.

-Daniel C. Haynes

JAMELL OGBONNA:

Jamell Ogbonna

With closed eyes, a soft prayer to the heavens, and a deep inhale, the world slips away. For a few seconds, nothing exists outside of the notes in his head. He's been here before though, and after a quick exhale, his fingers dance across the keys, filling the air with the robust, smooth sounds of the saxophone in his hands. It's more than a performance, it's something much deeper. For him, it's one word: "purpose". It's a purpose that has been redefined in the middle of a pandemic through a deeper relationship with God.

The case could be made that music has always been in 23-year-old Jamell Ogbonna's blood. With a Nigerian father and a Trinidadian mother, the sounds of soca, afro beats, reggae, and dancehall were constants in his homes. His parents met at Manhattan College in New York and called the city home. But a few years later when he was around five, Ogbonna moved to Georgia with his mom before living in Trinidad for a year, while his dad stayed in New York. After returning from Trinidad, he would spend much of his time going back and forth between Georgia and New York. "They're not together, but I still have a close relationship with both my parents; I go to my dad here in New York every weekend, and I have a good relationship with both sides of my family," Ogbonna said, pausing to think for a moment.

Looking back at it now, he believes that growing up in those two environments was important to not only his understanding of music, but his understanding of himself. "It wasn't just music but being exposed to a different sound and culture. I could associate myself with it." This association led him to join the school band in the sixth grade where he played the saxophone for the first time. Since the sixth grade, there has been

PURPOSE THROUGH MUSIC

Written by Daniel Haynes

Dec 6, 2020

a dedication to improving his craft. In his sophomore year of high school, he started with other instruments like the piano before getting into brass instruments a year later. Today, he plays the saxophone, piano, drums, harmonica, baritone, trombone, sings, and is currently learning to play the guitar proficiently.

Photos by Jamell Ogbonna

Despite the sax being his first love, it was the piano that led to a major turning point in his life while he was in college. "I went to St. John's University for my undergrad, and I was in Marillac auditorium when they had the piano," he said. "I was in there because I would go every Sunday and just play music." It would so happen that one Sunday while playing, members of the Christian group Eden would find Ogbonna playing and ask to use the room and the piano for practice. "They came through and said they wanted to use it for practice, and I was like sure. I walked out and something told me to go back, sit, and listen. They started playing gospel music and I played with them and actually joined their band. I started going to meetings and the rest is history."

In Eden, Ogbonna's spirituality would reach new heights. Growing up, he was a Catholic, but this is only because he was taken to church every weekend. When a teenager, and able to make his own choices, he became agnostic after religion got confusing to him. It wasn't until that Sunday in Marillac he would restart his spiritual journey by giving his heart to God. While at school, he would also join the Voices of Victory Gospel Choir where he would use his talents to glorify God.

"I heard this quote that said prayer is when I talk to God, meditation is when I listen, but with the piano I could do both, I like to say with music I could do both."

As his faith grew, so did his creativity and production rate. He recorded music and played live gigs sometimes with other artists at school, like Georgia rapper, Blake Breeze. This growing faith and music kept him going during the heights of the pandemic lockdowns. A graduating senior, a month away from his Bachelor of Science in Biology, when St. John's closed campus, Ogbonna turned to God and music. Living in an off-campus apartment meant he didn't have to pack everything and leave, and with the isolation, he could focus on music and plans for the future.

HEALING NOTES

""During the pandemic, all I've had is time to think," Ogbonna said in a somber tone. To this point, talking about life before the pandemic felt light and easy. His hands had moved excitedly while he spoke, and the smile on his face only left when he laughed at something he remembered.

Now, talking about the pandemic stretched the smile to a line and his hands rested on the desk in front of him. "My whole undergrad track, I was a bio-major, and the goal was to be a pediatrician with musical therapy applications in the future. But in isolation and as I grew in my faith and music, I realized it wasn't what I wanted to do anymore," he said.

"I thought about how I could still do music therapy and not just help pediatric but all the way to geriatric."

It's this clarity that caused him to go to Molloy College for grad school. At Molloy, he is doing his master's in music therapy where he's learning how to use music and psychology to heal people. "My whole undergrad track, I was a bio-major and the goal was to be a pediatrician with musical therapy applications in the future. But in isolation and as I grew in my faith and music, I realized it wasn't what I wanted to do anymore," he said.

He also works at Parker Jewish Institute in recreational therapy, music therapy, and therapeutic music. "It's an important part in the art of healing cause in the same way we use music to shift the atmosphere in church, is the same principle when trying to heal somebody from depression and suicidal thoughts or help with self-empowerment." The isolation also allowed Ogbonna to tap into his creativity.

Being at home and unable to perform live, he uploaded videos of himself playing pieces on Instagram. He also started collaborating with different artists. One of these artists was Randy Mason, a musician, and host of a music series called Quarantine Jams. "I think I was Quarantine Jams nine... like it was fun and a good culture, and it's allowing people to express themselves during these hard times and just be creative," he said, the smile returning to his face.

He would also perform a solo as a tribute to a close friend who got married during the pandemic. "The song I did is by her husband. I saw his post saying five more days till she was Mrs. Duruji on Instagram and I worked on the song for them and made sure I got it out the same day cause I couldn't be there due to social distancing."

In recent weeks, Ogbonna has been planning for his future. He wants to start shows, launch his own label to showcase and advocate for creatives and artists, and ultimately shift the culture. I asked him what music meant to him. A few seconds passed before he answered.

"It's life, it's art in one of its purest forms. It's creative, it's an expression, it's an experience, it's a gift, it's healing, it's communication, it's spiritual.

It's God's purpose for me."

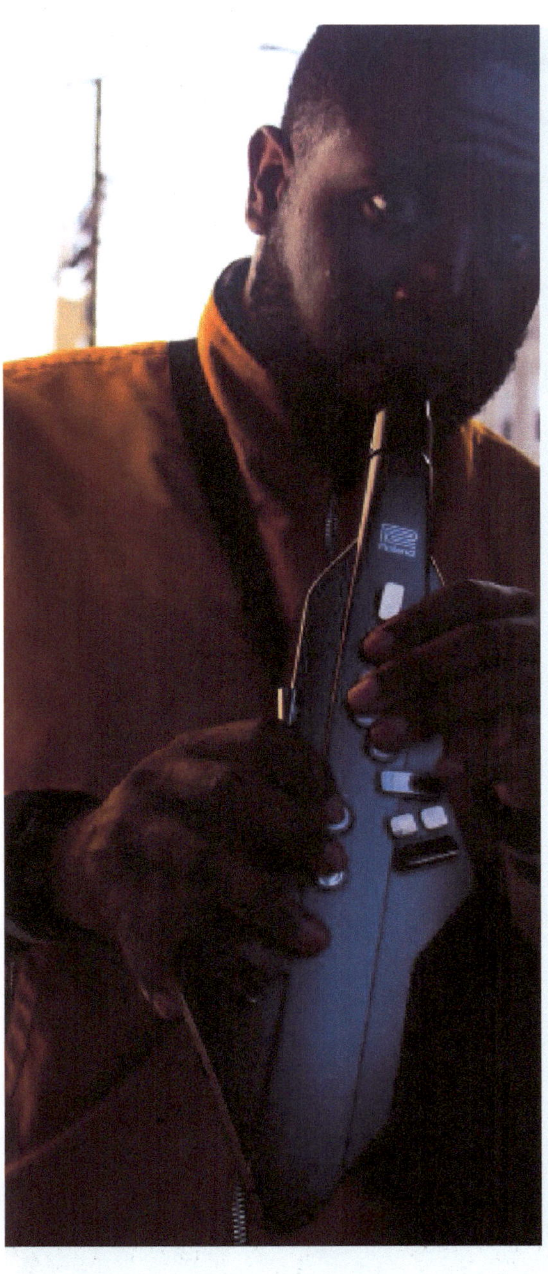
Roland

DAVE TURNER: BEYO

Dave Turner

When you first enter a barbershop, most times you are greeted with a feeling of comfort. Good conversation, great music, the immediate scent of talcum powder, and the steady hum of clippers fill the entire room. In our current environment, a barbershop stands as an oasis in a desert filled with politics and health dangers.

At the local Detroit shop The Grooming Room, you'll find the hands of Dave Turner smoothly draping the next customer in a cape that protects them from the world's problems-even if it's for an hour. With the flick of a switch, his clippers buzz to life. It's a familiar sound that's steady and soothing, and with every move hair drops to the floor, the steady buzz hinting at the mastery at work. For the last 14 years, Dave Turner has been a part of the oasis, changing the moods of clients one haircut at a time. Through the help of his brother, and the people he's met while barbering, Dave has been able to express his creativity in diverse ways, but barbering wasn't always a career goal

The Start of Something New

At the popular Downtown Detroit Michigan event center The Rooster Tail, Dave once was a pastry chef. His head chef had seen a drawing Turner did during his break on a napkin and moved him in order to let his creativity flourish. "Why the hell are you on my line when you can draw like this?" the chef had asked.

After moving departments, Dave used to make ice carvings and wedding cakes for a living. His event team was hired to cater a party for a player on the Pittsburgh Steelers during the 2006 Super Bowl in Detroit. Dave and the other chefs were excited for both the opportunities to connect with the team, and what it meant for their direct deposits. "When I got my check, I was so disappointed I went to the Executive Chef," said Dave. That same day he quit, and with no plan, he called his younger brother who told him to go to barber school. Two days later, he joined.

"Anyone that knows me knows it isn't about the money, it's about the experience of meeting new people, and learning stuff," said Dave. It's now been over a decade of cutting hair, and his motivation has not changed. He's still excited to see who lands in his chair next. "The judge, prosecutor, defendant everybody, and they're all on the same page... in this chair". His love for conversation, all while providing a superb barbering experience has introduced him to people that have helped him 'level up' his creativity. From painters and photographers to people going out on shows, to musicians talking about how long they've rehearsed, they're all the fuel to continue his work.

ND THE BARBER'S CHAIR

Written by Alexander Coger-Bonet

Mar 2, 2021

Dave the Creative

"I paint and draw a lot, and I needed a reference to go off of...so I thought to myself, man if I got a camera, I could take pictures of stuff I wanted to draw," said Dave. And for a while, that was enough for Turner. Sometime later, he was called into a studio for a local video shoot. He would cut the hair of his friend Marcus Devine, and others on the set. When he finished, he was welcomed to stay and see the video being completed.

"When [Marcus] pulled out that camera I said yo! that's the same one as mine, he asked me why aren't I making any money?" It was a question that stuck with him, and he went straight home and dove into the internet, looking to learn about his camera and what it could do. He discovered that photography, and videography is an art in itself. After he sold his first photoprint, he knew he could do it more. This fascination developed into photo gigs, a documentary called Barber Life 313, and a YouTube channel called 'Dave the People's Barber TV'.

On his channel he covers a number of topics like paying attention to going to a licensed barber, health precautions, product recommendations and the motivation to keep working. "I knew that I had achieved some level of excellence when people trusted me to be their photographer at their wedding."

A Vet in the Game

"Everything you can think of in the barbering game I've done it before." From being flown out to cut clients hair, owning his own barber shop, working with famous clients, the list goes on for Dave. He could be considered a 'celebrity barber', but that label is something he wants to avoid. He appreciates "the guy at the plant that comes to kick it every two weeks and pays" over "some dude in a movie."

One of the things you get from 15 years of barbering is countless stories. He told one about Carl Anthony Payne II, the actor who played Cole on the popular show Martin and the time he tried to skate out on paying the bill. Carl was a part of a play in Detroit some years ago, one that Dave was invited to handle the hair needs of the cast. When Payne tried to use his fame as a method of payment, Dave said "Hold on bro you need to magically make my money appear." After watching Payne scramble to find someone else to pay for his haircut before the play of everyday people.

His coworkers and friends proclaim Dave to be a modern-day renaissance man. Drawing, painting, photography, videography, guitar, and barbering are a lot to ask of any man, despite Dave Turner saying the opposite. For him? "Art is my whole life...It's all the same, you need to have the tools and know what to do with them, it's all appealing to the eye and starts a conversation."

IZDIGO:

SOUTH ORANGE'S

VERY OWN

Written by Daniel Haynes

February 2019

Photo Credits: Izdigo

As he cruises through the Ville in South Orange New Jersey with his windows down, the voice of Nipsey Hussle blasts through his speakers. "All my life, been grindin' all my life, sacrificed, hustled, paid the price" he raps along with the late crenshaw rapper. His camera equipment is on the backseat, and as he hits every word on the beat there's an underlying sense of truth to the lyrics the 23-year-old Isaiah Gill is rapping along to.

Currently sitting on 9k followers, the New Jersey native has amassed a following largely in part to this photo taken three and a half years ago. As he recounts it, he can't help but shake his head with a slight smile. "I took a photo of one of my good friends, a RnB singer Golden Moonchild, she hit me up and asked to do a shoot for her like let's just go outside and take some pictures and it was just normal," he says. That normalcy was the calm before the social media rainstorm Gill was about to experience a few hours later. "As I took the photos, I showed her and I said I think we on to something here and I went home edited the pictures and posted it" he adds.

Gill was indeed on to something and the next morning when he woke up his dms (direct messages) were overflowing with what he calls love. "I woke up and mad people started hitting me up like your work is crazy and at that moment I didn't know how impactful my art was and people started telling me that the image inspired them to start photography."

He says the next thing that came was people from across the world asking him about the camera he used and "all that boring stuff, well boring to them, not to me."

For Gill photography has been life-changing, the first of those changes came back in 2015 when he was referred to an artist named IamG. It was this connection that helped him learn and build his network. "He liked my artwork a lot and he asked me if I wanted to go on tour with them and at first, I didn't know what to say but um I was young and I said fuck it let's do it and I ended up going on tour that following week", said Gill nonchalantly.

"G was going on tour with Mike Stud at the time and he wanted a photographer to go with him on the tour and snap some dope shots and Iz was honestly the dopest photographer around at the time and he got brought out on tour and that's just how it came about" said long time best friend Denzel Wilson. Wilson was the one who connected Gill to IamG. He's been one of Gill's best friends since their senior year of high school and has been the subject of many of his photos. It wasn't always "picture perfect" for Gill though, and his lenses weren't always focused. He went through what he calls learning lessons for him to get to this point. Being very candid he started to explain.

"I hit a couple dead ends very early on, but that's all part of the learning process" he said, "I struggled getting money to pay for pictures and during that time when there's nothing, I'd just get a parttime job to keep funding my craft regardless of what it was," he said with a sort of casual shrug that belied the experiences of the young photographer.

It's that dedication to his craft that caused Gill to see photography not as a job, but always more of an avenue to express himself as an artist. It's been the creativity, the natural eye for angles, lights and things others don't see as well as the love for the thing that was a constant throughout everything, he's gone through that makes it enjoyable.

It feels like it's all come full circle for Gill as we sit in his living room. His father also a photographer is the one who set Gill on the path he is on now from when he first picked up the camera in 2013 and walked outside to take an album cover photo in a Chicken Shack near his house.

"Before I even started thinking of photography, I was a rapper in high school, and I started it because the homies wanted an album cover, and I was the only one with a camera. I did one photo for them and instead of going inside I stopped outside the Chicken Shack and took a picture of them through the window. I took it home and showed my father and he was the one who had given me his camera; he told me I had a gift and to keep going."

It's that ability to keep going that has amazed Wilson. "Just watching him grow as an artist and seeing where he is at now, I definitely expected but it's amazing that it became a reality... watching him become who he is, watching him become Izdigo. He's went through many different phases, and I think all the phases he's been through he took knowledge from and applied it to his life and how he thinks."

Sentiments echoed by another one of Gill's friends HueGo, "It has truly been a pleasure to witness each transition," One of the great things about how Isaiah has grown was his ability to maintain his core values and personality traits which make him one of a kind." "No matter the crowd he was with, or the medium he chose to express himself, the things that made him who he is always remained intact", continued HueGo.

What Gill has his eyes set on now and in the future is having fun with his craft. He doesn't have any direct end goal in mind, and it's something he's comfortable with. He's founded his own website, produced his own merchandise, been on tour with rappers, and turned one of his passions and constants into a life.

When asked what he knew was a certainty he laid back in his chair, put his feet up on the table and laughed before saying, "I do know that whenever I retire imma have my own record shop and be an art professor...fuck it why not."

What am I supposed to do when I feel so helpless
Like I'm trapped beneath the waves, struggling to reach the surface.
Everything in me screaming, but no sound from my mouth like I'm mute.
But I'm not mute I'm dumb,
no fuck it
I'm numb.

Numb to the pain, numb to the anger.
This Pain like novacain, in my mouth that got me too numb to speak.
I'm out here carrying the world on my shoulders but even Atlas feels weak.
I want to put the world down for just one second,
But there ain't no peace, there ain't no retreat,
there ain't no safe space or safe place cause
real life don't play that soft shit.

Stand up boy, fix your lips together,
let that firm line
stay for all time cause,
you a man and you ain't supposed to show no fear or show no weakness,
ain't nobody ask for a lil bitch.

But I'm a Black man dying and we got feelings too...

-Daniel Haynes
May 31, 2020

Photo by Luana Seu

US

www.ingramcontent.com/pod-product-compliance
Lightning Source LLC
LaVergne TN
LVHW070134110826
845147LV00002B/250
* 9 7 9 8 9 8 9 9 5 9 8 3 9 *